BITS OF TALK

ABOUT HOME MATTERS.

ABOUT HOME MATTERS.

By H. H.,
AUTHOR OF "VERSES" AND "BITS OF TRAVEL."

BOSTON:
ROBERTS BROTHERS.
1873.

CAMBRIDGE:

PRESS OF JOHN WILSON AND SON.

CONTENTS.

BITS OF TALK.

THE INHUMANITIES OF PARENTS.

CORPORAL PUNISHMENT.

NOT long ago a Presbyterian minister in Western New York whipped his three-year-old boy to death, for refusing to say his prayers. The little fingers were broken; the tender flesh was bruised and actually mangled; strong men wept when they looked on the body; and the reverend murderer, after having been set free on bail, was glad to return and take refuge within the walls of his prison, to escape summary punishment at the hands of an outraged community. At the bare mention of such cruelty, every heart grew sick and faint; men and women were dumb with horror: only tears and a hot demand for instant retaliation availed.

The question whether, after all, that baby martyr were not fortunate among his fellows, would, no doubt, be met by resentful astonishment. But it is a question which may well be asked, may well be pondered. Heart-rending as it is to think for an instant of the agonies which the poor child must have borne for some hours after his infant brain was too bewildered by terror and pain to understand what was required of him, it still cannot fail to occur to deeper reflection that the torture was short and small in comparison with what the next ten years might have held for him if he had lived. To earn entrance on the spiritual life by the briefest possible experience of the physical, is always "greater gain;" but how emphatically is it so when the conditions of life upon earth are sure to be unfavorable!

If it were possible in any way to get a statistical summing-up and a tangible presentation of the amount of physical pain inflicted by parents on children under twelve years of age, the most callous-hearted would be surprised and shocked. If it were possible to add to this estimate an accurate and scientific demonstration of the extent to which such pain, by weakening the nervous system and exhausting its capacity to resist disease, diminishes children's chances for life, the world would stand aghast.

Too little has been said upon this point. The opponents of corporal punishment usually approach the subject either from the sentimental or the moral standpoint. The argument on either of these grounds can be made strong enough, one would suppose, to paralyze every hand lifted to strike a child. But the question of the direct and lasting physical effect of blows — even of one blow on the delicate tissues of a child's body, on the frail and trembling nerves, on the sensitive organization which is trying, under a thousand unfavoring conditions, to adjust itself to the hard work of both living and growing — has yet to be properly considered.

Every one knows the sudden sense of insupportable pain, sometimes producing even dizziness and nausea, which follows the accidental hitting of the ankle or elbow against a hard substance. It does not need that the blow be very hard to bring involuntary tears to adult eyes. But what is such a pain as this, in comparison with the pain of a dozen or more quick tingling blows from a heavy hand on flesh which is, which must be as much more sensitive than ours, as are the souls which dwell in it purer than ours. Add to this physical pain the overwhelming terror which only utter helplessness can feel, and which is the most recognizable quality in the cry of a very young child under whipping; add the instinctive sense of disgrace, of outrage, which often keeps the older child stubborn and still throughout, — and you have an amount and an intensity of suffering from which even tried nerves might shrink. Again, who does not know — at least, what woman does not know — that violent weeping, for even a very short time, is quite enough to cause a feeling of languor and depression, of nervous exhaustion for a whole day? Yet it does not seem to occur to mothers that little children must feel this, in proportion to the length of time and violence of their crying, far more than grown people. Who has not often seen a poor child receive, within an hour or two of the first whipping, a second one, for some small ebullition of nervous irritability, which was simply inevitable from its spent and worn condition?

It is safe to say that in families where whipping is regularly recognized as a punishment, few children under ten years of age, and of average behavior, have less than one whipping a week. Sometimes they have more, sometimes the whipping is very severe. Thus you have in one short year sixty or seventy occasions on which for a greater or less time, say from one to three hours, the child's nervous system is subjected to a tremendous strain from the effect of terror and physical pain combined with long crying. Will any physician tell us that this fact is not an element in that child's physical condition at the end of that year? Will any physician dare to say that there may not be, in that child's life, crises when the issues of life and death will be so equally balanced that the tenth part of the nervous force lost in such fits of crying, and in the endurance of such pain, could turn the scale?

Nature's retributions, like her rewards, are cumulative. Because her sentences against evil works are not executed speedily, therefore the hearts of the sons of men are fully set in them to do evil. But the sentence always is executed, sooner or later, and that inexorably. Your son, O unthinking mother! may fall by the way in the full prime of his manhood, for lack of that strength which his infancy spent in enduring your hasty and severe punishments.

It is easy to say, — and universally is said, — by people who cling to the old and fight against the new,

"All this outcry about corporal punishment is sentimental nonsense. The world is full of men and women, who have grown up strong and good, in spite of whippings; and as for me, I know I never had any more whipping than I deserved, or than was good for me."

Are you then so strong and clear and pure in your physical and spiritual nature and life, that you are sure no different training could have made either your body or your soul better? Are these men and women, of whom the world is full, so able-bodied, whole-souled, strong-minded, that you think it needless to look about for any method of making the next generation better? Above all, do you believe that it is a part of the legitimate outworking of God's plan and intent in creating human beings to have more than one-half of them die in childhood? If we are not to believe that this fearful mortality is a part of God's plan, is it wise to refuse to consider all possibilities, even those seemingly most remote, of diminishing it?

No argument is so hard to meet (simply because it is not an argument) as the assumption of the good and propriety of "the thing that hath been." It is one of the devil's best sophistries, by which he keeps good people undisturbed in doing the things he likes. It has been in all ages the bulwark behind which evils have made stand, and have slain their thousands. It is the last enemy which shall be destroyed. It is the only real support of the cruel evil of corporal punishment.

Suppose that such punishment of children had been unheard of till now. Suppose that the idea had yesterday been suggested for the first time that by inflicting physical pain on a child's body you might make him recollect certain truths; and suppose that instead of whipping, a very moderate and harmless degree of pricking with pins or cutting with knives or burning with fire had been suggested. Would not fathers and mothers have cried out all over the land at the inhumanity of the idea?

Would they not still cry out at the inhumanity of one who, as things are to-day, should propose the substitution of pricking or cutting or burning for whipping? But I think it would not be easy to show in what wise small pricks or cuts are more inhuman than blows; or why lying may not be as legitimately cured by blisters made with a hot coal as by black and blue spots made with a ruler. The principle is the same; and if the principle be right, why not multiply methods?

It seems as if this one suggestion, candidly considered, might be enough to open all parents' eyes to the enormity of whipping. How many a loving mother will, without any thought of cruelty, inflict half-a-dozen quick blows on the little hand of her child, when she could no more take a pin and make the same number of thrusts into the tender flesh, than she could bind the baby on a rack. Yet the pin-thrusts would hurt far less, and would probably make a deeper impression on the child's mind.

Among the more ignorant classes, the frequency and

severity of corporal punishment of children, are appalling. The facts only need to be held up closely and persistently before the community to be recognized as horrors of cruelty far greater than some which have been made subjects of legislation.

It was my misfortune once to be forced to spend several of the hottest weeks of a hot summer in New York. In near neighborhood to my rooms were blocks of buildings which had shops on the first floor and tenements above. In these lived the families of small tradesmen, and mechanics of the better sort. During those scorching nights every window was thrown open, and all sounds were borne with distinctness through the hot still air. Chief among them were the shrieks and cries of little children, and blows and angry words from tired, overworked mothers. At times it became almost unbearable: it was hard to refrain from an attempt at rescue. Ten, twelve, twenty quick, hard blows, whose sound rang out plainly, I counted again and again; mingling with them came the convulsive screams of the poor children, and that most piteous thing of all, the reiteration of "Oh, mamma! oh, mamma!" as if, through all, the helpless little creatures had an instinct that this word ought to be in itself the strongest appeal. These families were all of the better class of work people, comfortable and respectable. What sounds were to be heard in the more wretched haunts of the city, during those nights, the heart struggled away from fancying. But the shrieks of those children will never wholly die out of the air. I hear them to-day; and mingling with them, the question rings perpetually in my ears, "Why does not the law protect children, before the point at which life is endangered?"

A cartman may be arrested in the streets for the brutal beating of a horse which is his own, and which he has the right to kill if he so choose. Should not a man be equally withheld from the brutal beating of a child who is not his own, but God's, and whom to kill is murder?

THE INHUMANITIES OF PARENTS.

NEEDLESS DENIALS.

WEBSTER'S Dictionary, which cannot be accused of any leaning toward sentimentalism, defines "inhumanity" as "cruelty in action;" and "cruelty" as "any act of a human being which inflicts unnecessary pain." The word inhumanity has an ugly sound, and many inhuman people are utterly and honestly unconscious of their own inhumanities; it is necessary therefore to entrench one's self behind some such bulwark as the above definitions afford, before venturing the accusation that fathers and mothers are habitually guilty of inhuman conduct in inflicting "unnecessary pain" on their children, by needless denials of their innocent wishes and impulses.

Most men and a great many women would be astonished at being told that simple humanity requires them to gratify every wish, even the smallest, of their children, when the pain of having that wish denied is not made necessary, either for the child's own welfare, physical or mental, or by circumstances beyond the parent's control. The word "necessary" is a very authoritative one; conscience, if left free, soon narrows down its boundaries; inconvenience, hindrance, deprivation, self-denial, one or all, or even a great deal of all, to ourselves, cannot give us a shadow of right to say that the pain of the child's disappointment is "necessary." Selfishness grasps at help from the hackneyed sayings, that it is "best for children to bear the yoke in their youth;" "the sooner they learn that they cannot have their own way the better;" "it is a good discipline for them to practise self-denial," &c. But the yoke that they *must* bear, in spite of our lightening it all we can, is heavy enough; the instances in which it is, for good and sufficient reasons, impossible for them to have their own way are quite numerous enough to insure their learning the lesson very early; and as for the discipline of self-denial, — God bless their dear, patient souls! — if men and women brought to bear on the thwartings and vexations of their daily lives, and their relations with each other, one hundredth part of the sweet acquiescence and brave endurance which average children show, under the average management of average parents, this world would be a much pleasanter place to live in than it is.

Let any conscientious and tender mother, who perhaps reads these words with tears half of resentment, half of grief in her eyes, keep for three days an exact record of the little requests which she refuses, from the baby of five, who begged to stand on a chair and look out of the window, and was hastily told, "No, it would hurt the chair," when one minute would have been enough time to lay a folded newspaper over the upholstery, and another minute enough to explain to him, with a kiss and a hug, "that that was to save his spoiling mamma's nice chair with his boots;" and the two minutes together would probably have made sure that another time the dear little fellow would look out for a paper himself, when he wished to climb up to the window, — from this baby up to the pretty girl of twelve, who, with as distinct a perception of the becoming as her mother had before her, went to school unhappy because she was compelled to wear the blue necktie instead of the scarlet one, and surely for no especial reason! At the end of the three days, an honest examination of the record would show that full half of these small denials, all of which had involved pain, and some of which had brought contest and punishment, had been needless, had been hastily made, and made usually on account of the slight interruption or inconvenience which would result from yielding to the request. I am very much mistaken if the honest keeping and honest study of such a three days' record would not wholly change the atmosphere in many a house to what it ought to be, and bring almost constant sunshine and bliss where now, too often, are storm and misery.

With some parents, although they are neither harsh nor hard in manner, nor yet unloving in nature, the habitual first impulse seems to be to refuse: they appear to have a singular obtuseness to the fact that it is, or can be, of any consequence to a child whether it does or does not do the thing it desires. Often the refusal is withdrawn on the first symptom of grief or disappointment on the child's part; a thing which is fatal to all real control of a child, and almost as unkind as the first unnecessary denial, — perhaps even more so, as it involves double and treble pains, in future instances, where there cannot and must not be any giving way to entreaties. It is doubtless this lack of perception, — akin, one would think, to color-blindness, — which is at the bottom of this great and common inhumanity among kind and intelligent fathers and mothers: an inhumanity so common that it may almost be said to be universal; so common that, while we are obliged to look on and see our dearest friends guilty of it, we find it next to impossible to make them understand what we mean when we make outcry over some of its glaring instances.

You, my dearest of friends, — or, rather, you who would be, but for this one point of hopeless contention between us, — do you remember a certain warm morning, last August, of which I told you then you had not heard the last? Here it is again · perhaps in print I can make it look blacker to you than I could then; part of it I saw, part of it you unwillingly confessed to me, and part of it little Blue Eyes told me herself.

It was one of those ineffable mornings, when a thrill of delight and expectancy fills the air; one felt that every appointment of the day must be unlike those of other days, — must be festive, must help on the "white day" for which all things looked ready. I remember how like the morning itself you looked as you stood in the doorway, in a fresh white muslin dress, with lavender ribbons. I said, "Oh, extravagance! For breakfast!"

"I know," you said; "but the day was so enchanting, I could not make up my mind to wear any thing that had been worn before." Here an uproar from the nursery broke out, and we both ran to the spot. There stood little Blue Eyes, in a storm of temper, with one small foot on a crumpled mass of pink cambric on the floor; and nurse, who was also very red and angry, explained that Miss would not have on her pink frock because it was not quite clean. "It is all dirty, mamma, and I don't want to put it on! You've got on a nice white dress: why can't I?"

You are in the main a kind mother, and you do not like to give little Blue Eyes pain; so you knelt down beside her, and told her that she must be a good girl, and have on the gown Mary had said, but that she should have on a pretty white apron, which would hide the spots. And Blue Eyes, being only six years old, and of a loving, generous nature, dried her tears, accepted the very questionable expedient, tried to forget the spots, and in a few moments came out on the piazza, chirping like a little bird. By this time the rare quality of the morning had stolen like wine into our brains, and you exclaimed, "We will have breakfast out here, under the vines! How George will like it!" And in another instant you were flitting back and forth, helping the rather ungracious Bridget move out the breakfast-table, with its tempting array.

"Oh, mamma, mamma," cried Blue Eyes, "can't I have my little tea-set on a little table beside your big table? Oh, let me, let me!" and she fairly quivered with excitement. You hesitated. How I watched you! But it was a little late. Bridget was already rather cross; the tea-set was packed in a box, and up on a high shelf.

"No, dear. There is not time, and we must not make Bridget any more trouble; but" — seeing the tears coming again — "you shall have some real tea in papa's big gilt cup, and another time you shall have your tea-set when we have breakfast out here again." As I said before, you are a kind mother, and you made the denial as easy to be borne as you could, and Blue Eyes was again pacified, not satisfied, only bravely making the best of it. And so we had our breakfast; a breakfast to be remembered, too. But as for the "other time" which you had promised to Blue Eyes; how well I knew that not many times a year did such mornings and breakfasts come, and that it was well she would forget all about it! After breakfast, — you remember how we lingered, — George suddenly started up, saying, "How hard it is to go to town! I say, girls, walk down to the station with me, both of you."

"And me too, me too, papa!" said Blue Eyes. You did not hear her; but I did, and she had flown for her hat. At the door we found her, saying again, "Me too, mamma!" Then you remembered her boots: "Oh, my darling," you said, kissing her, for you are a kind mother, " you cannot go in those nice boots: the dew will spoil them; and it is not worth while to change them, we shall be back in a few minutes."

A storm of tears would have burst out in an instant at this the third disappointment, if I had not sat down on the door-step, and, taking her in my lap, whispered that auntie was going to stay too.

"Oh, put the child down, and come along," called the great, strong, uncomprehending man — Blue Eyes' dear papa. "Pussy won't mind. Be a good girl, pussy; I'll bring you a red balloon to-night."

You are both very kind, you and George, and you both love little Blue Eyes dearly.

"No, I won't come. I believe my boots are too thin," said I; and for the equivocation there was in my reply I am sure of being forgiven. You both turned back twice to look at the child, and kissed your hands to her; and I wondered if you did not see in her face, what I did, real grief and patient endurance. Even "The King of the Golden River" did not rouse her: she did not want a story; she did not want me; she did not want a red balloon at night; she wanted to walk between you, to the station, with her little hands in yours! God grant the day may not come when you will be heart-broken because you can never lead her any more!

She asked me some questions, while you were gone, which you remember I repeated to you. She asked me if I did not hate nice new shoes; and why little girls could not put on the dresses they liked best; and if mamma did not look beautiful in that pretty white dress; and said that, if she could only have had her own tea-set, at breakfast, she would have let me have my coffee in one of her cups. Gradually she grew happier, and began to tell me about her great wax-doll, which had eyes that could shut; which was kept in a trunk because she was too little, mamma said, to play very much with it now; but she guessed mamma would let her have it to-day; did I not think so? Alas! I did, and I said so; in fact, I felt sure that it was the very thing you would be certain to do, to sweeten the day, which had begun so sadly for poor little Blue Eyes.

It seemed very long to her before you came back, and she was on the point of asking for her dolly as soon as you appeared; but I whispered to her to wait till you were rested. After a few minutes I took her up to your room, — that lovely room with the bay window to the east; there you sat, in your white dress, surrounded with gay worsteds, all looking like a carnival of humming-birds. "Oh, how beautiful!" I exclaimed, in involuntary admiration; "what are you doing?" You said that you were going to make an affghan, and that the morning was so enchanting you could not bear the thought of touching your mending, but were going to luxuriate in the worsteds. Some time passed in sorting the colors, and deciding on the contrasts, and I forgot all about the doll. Not so little Blue Eyes. I remembered afterward how patiently she stood still, waiting and waiting for a gap between our words, that she need not break the law against interrupting, with her eager—

"Please, mamma, let me have my wax dolly to play with this morning! I'll sit right here on the floor, by you and auntie, and not hurt her one bit. Oh, please do, mamma!"

You mean always to be a very kind mother, and you spoke as gently and lovingly as it is possible to speak when you replied:—

"Oh, Pussy, mamma is too busy to get it; she can't get up now. You can play with your blocks, and with your other dollies, just as well; that's a good little girl."

Probably, if Blue Eyes had gone on imploring, you would have laid your worsteds down, and given her the dolly; for you love her dearly, and never mean to make her unhappy. But neither you nor I were prepared for what followed.

"You're a naughty, ugly, hateful mamma! You never let me do *any* thing, and I wish you were dead!" with such a burst of screaming and tears that we were both frightened. You looked, as well you might, heart-broken at such words from your only child. You took her away; and when you came back, you cried, and said you had whipped her severely, and you did not know what you should do with a child of such a frightful temper.

"Such an outburst as that, just because I told her, in the gentlest way possible, that she could not have a plaything! It is terrible!"

Then I said some words to you, which you thought were unjust. I asked you in what condition your own nerves would have been by ten o'clock that morning if your husband (who had, in one view, a much better right to thwart your harmless desires than you had to thwart your child's, since you, in the full understanding of maturity, gave yourself into his hands) had, instead of admiring your pretty white dress, told you to be more prudent, and not put it on; had told you it would be nonsense to have breakfast out on the piazza; and that he could not wait for you to walk to the station with him. You said that the cases were not at all parallel; and I replied hotly that that was very true, for those matters would have been to you only the comparative trifles of one short day, and would have made you only a little cross and uncomfortable; whereas to little Blue Eyes they were the all-absorbing desires of the hour, which, to a child in trouble, always looks as if it could never come to an end, and would never be followed by any thing better.

Blue Eyes cried herself to sleep, and slept heavily till late in the afternoon. When her father came home, you said that she must not have the red balloon, because she had been such a naughty girl. I have wondered many times since why she did not cry again, or look grieved when you said that, and laid the balloon away. After eleven o'clock at night, I went to look at her, and found her sobbing in her sleep, and tossing about. I groaned as I thought, "This is only one day, and there are three hundred and sixty-five in a year!" But I never recall the distorted face of that poor child, as, in her fearful passion, she told you she wished you were dead, without also remembering that even the gentle Christ said of him who should offend one of these little ones, "It were better for him that a mill-stone were hanged about his neck, and he were drowned in the depths of the sea!"

THE INHUMANITIES OF PARENTS.

RUDENESS.

"*Inhumanity* — Cruelty. *Cruelty* — The disposition to give unnecessary pain." — *Webster's Dict.*

I HAD intended to put third on the list of inhumanities of parents "needless requisitions;" but my last summer's observations changed my estimate, and convinced me that children suffer more pain from the rudeness with which they are treated than from being forced to do needless things which they dislike. Indeed, a positively and graciously courteous manner toward children is a thing so rarely seen in average daily life, the rudenesses which they receive are so innumerable, that it is hard to tell where to begin in setting forth the evil. Children themselves often bring their sharp and unexpected logic to bear on some incident illustrating the difference in this matter of behavior between what is required from them and what is shown to them: as did a little boy I knew, whose father said crossly to him one morning, as he came into the breakfast-room, "Will you ever learn to shut that door after you?" and a few seconds later, as the child was rather sulkily sitting down in his chair,

"And do you mean to bid anybody 'good-morning,' or not?" "I don't think you gave *me* a very nice 'good-morning,' anyhow," replied satirical justice, aged seven. Then, of course, he was reproved for speaking disrespectfully; and so in the space of three minutes the beautiful opening of the new day, for both parents and children, was jarred and robbed of its fresh harmony by the father's thoughtless rudeness.

Was the breakfast-room door much more likely to be shut the next morning? No. The lesson was pushed aside by the pain, the motive to resolve was dulled by the antagonism. If that father had called his son, and, putting his arm round him, (oh! the blessed and magic virtue of putting your arm round a child's neck!) had said, "Good-morning, my little man;" and then, in a confidential whisper in his ear, "What shall we do to make this forgetful little boy remember not to leave that door open, through which the cold wind blows in on all of us?" — can any words measure the difference between the first treatment and the second? between the success of the one and the failure of the other?

Scores of times in a day, a child is told, in a short, authoritative way, to do or not to do such little things as we ask at the hands of older people, as favors, graciously, and with deference to their choice. "Would you be so very kind as to close that window?" "May I trouble you for that cricket?" "If you would be as comfortable in this chair as in that, I would like to change places with you." "Oh, excuse me, but your head is between me and the light: could you see as well if you moved a little?" "Would it hinder you too long to stop at the store for me? I would be very much obliged to you, if you would." "Pray, do not let me crowd you," &c. In most people's speech to children, we find, as synonyms for these polite phrases: "Shut that window down, this minute." "Bring me that cricket." "I want that chair; get up. You can sit in this." "Don't you see that you are right in my light? Move along." "I want you to leave off playing, and go right down to the store for me." "Don't crowd so. Can't you see that there is not room enough for two people here?" and so on. As I write, I feel an instinctive consciousness that these sentences will come like home-thrusts to some surprised people. I hope so. That is what I want. I am sure that in more than half the cases where family life is marred in peace, and almost stripped of beauty, by just these little rudenesses, the parents are utterly unconscious of them. The truth is, it has become like an established custom, this different and less courteous way of speaking to children on small occasions and minor matters. People who are generally civil and of fair kindliness do it habitually, not only to their own children, but to all children. We see it in the cars, in the stages, in stores, in Sunday schools, everywhere.

On the other hand, let a child ask for any thing without saying "please," receive any thing without saying "thank you," sit still in the most comfortable seat without offering to give it up, or press its own preference for a particular book, chair, or apple, to the inconveniencing of an elder, and what an outcry we have: "Such rudeness!" "Such an ill-mannered child!" "His parents must have neglected him strangely." Not at all: they have been steadily telling him a great many times every day not to do these precise things which you dislike. But they themselves have been all the while doing those very things to him; and there is no proverb which strikes a truer balance between two things than the old one which weighs example over against precept.

However, that it is bad policy to be rude to children is the least of the things to be said against it. Over this they will triumph, sooner or later. The average healthy child has a native bias towards gracious good behavior and kindly affections. He will win and be won in the long run, and, the chances are, have better manners than his father. But the pain that we give these blessed little ones when we wound their tenderness, — for that there is no atoning. Over that they can never triumph, either now or hereafter. Why do we dare to be so sure that they are not grieved by ungracious words and tones? that they can get used to being continually treated as if they were "in the way"? Who has not heard this said? I have, until I have longed for an Elijah and for fire, that the grown-up cumberers of the ground, who are the ones really in the way, might be burned up, to make room for the children. I believe that, if it were possible to count up in any one month, and show in the aggregate, all of this class of miseries borne by children, the world would cry out astonished. I know a little girl, ten years old, of nervous temperament, whose whole physical condition is disordered, and seriously, by her mother's habitual atmosphere of rude fault-finding. She is a sickly, fretful, unhappy, almost unbearable child. If she lives to grow up, she will be a sickly, fretful, unhappy, unlovely woman. But her mother is just as much responsible for the whole as if she had deranged her system by feeding her on poisonous drugs. Yet she is a most conscientious, devoted, and anxious mother, and, in spite of this manner, a loving one. She does not know that there is any better way than hers. She does not see that her child is mortified and harmed when she says to her, in the presence of strangers, "How do you suppose you *look* with your mouth open like that?" "Do you want me to show you how you are sitting?"—and then a grotesque imitation of her stooping shoulders. "*Will* you sit still for one minute?" "*Do* take your hands off my dress." "Was there ever such an awkward child?" When the child replies fretfully and disagreeably, she does not see that it is only an exact reflection of her own voice and manners. She does not understand any of the things that would make for her own peace, as well as for the child's. Matters grow worse, instead of better, as the child grows older and has more will; and the chances are that the poor little soul will be worried into her grave.

Probably most parents, even very kindly ones, would

be a little startled at the assertion that a child ought never to be reproved in the presence of others. This is so constant an occurrence that nobody thinks of noticing it; nobody thinks of considering whether it be right and best, or not. But it is a great rudeness to a child. I am entirely sure that it ought never to be done. Mortification is a condition as unwholesome as it is uncomfortable. When the wound is inflicted by the hand of a parent, it is all the more certain to rankle and do harm. Let a child see that his mother is so anxious that he should have the approbation and good-will of her friends that she will not call their attention to his faults; and that, while she never, under any circumstances, allows herself to forget to tell him afterward, alone, if he has behaved improperly, she will spare him the additional pain and mortification of public reproof; and, while that child will lay these secret reproofs to heart, he will still be happy.

I know a mother who had the insight to see this, and the patience to make it a rule; for it takes far more patience, far more time, than the common method.

She said sometimes to her little boy, after visitors had left the parlor, "Now, dear, I am going to be your little girl, and you are to be my papa. And we will play that a gentleman has just come in to see you, and I will show you exactly how you have been behaving while this lady has been calling to see me. And you can see if you do not feel very sorry to have your little girl behave so."

Here is a dramatic representation at once which that boy does not need to see repeated many times before he is forever cured of interrupting, of pulling his mother's gown, of drumming on the piano, &c., — of the thousand and one things which able-bodied children can do to make social visiting where they are a martyrdom and a penance.

Once I saw this same little boy behave so boisterously and rudely at the dinner-table, in the presence of guests, that I said to myself, " Surely, this time she will have to break her rule, and reprove him publicly." I saw several telegraphic signals of rebuke, entreaty, and warning flash from her gentle eyes to his ; but nothing did any good. Nature was too much for him ; he could not at that minute force himself to be quiet. Presently she said, in a perfectly easy and natural tone, " Oh, Charley, come here a minute ; I want to tell you something." No one at the table supposed that it had any thing to do with his bad behavior. She did not intend that they should. As she whispered to him, I alone saw his cheek flush, and that he looked quickly and imploringly into her face ; I alone saw that tears were almost in her eyes. But she shook her head, and he went back to his seat with a manful but very red little face. In a few moments he laid down his knife and fork, and said, " Mamma, will you please to excuse me ? " " Certainly, my dear," said she. Nobody but I understood it, or observed that the little fellow had to run very fast to get out of the room without crying. Afterward she told me that she never sent a child away from the table in any other way. "But what would you do," said I, "if he were to refuse to ask to be excused?" Then the tears stood full in her eyes. "Do you think he could," she replied, "when he sees that I am only trying to save him from pain?" In the evening, Charley sat in my lap, and was very sober. At last he whispered to me, "I'll tell you an awful secret, if you won't tell. Did you think I had done my dinner this afternoon when I got excused? Well, I hadn't. Mamma made me, because I acted so. That's the way she always does. But I haven't had to have it done to me before for ever so long, — not since I was a little fellow" (he was eight now); "and I don't believe I ever shall again till I'm a man." Then he added, reflectively, "Mary brought me all the rest of my dinner upstairs; but I wouldn't touch it, only a little bit of the ice-cream. I don't think I deserved any at all; do you?"

I shall never, so long as I live, forget a lesson of this sort which my own mother once gave me. I was not more than seven years old; but I had a great susceptibility to color and shape in clothes, and an insatiable admiration for all people who came finely dressed. One day, my mother said to me, "Now I will play 'house' with you." Who does not remember when to "play house" was their chief of plays? And to whose later thought has it not occurred that in this mimic little show lay bound up the whole of life? My mother was the liveliest of playmates, she took the worst doll, the broken tea-set. the shabby furniture, and the least convenient corner of the room for her establishment. Social life became a round of festivities when she kept house as my opposite neighbor. At last, after the washing-day, and the baking-day, and the day when she took dinner with me, and the day when we took our children and walked out together, came the day for me to take my oldest child and go across to make a call at her house. Chill discomfort struck me on the very threshold of my visit. Where was the genial, laughing, talking lady who had been my friend up to that moment? There she sat, stock-still, dumb, staring first at my bonnet, then at my shawl, then at my gown, then at my feet; up and down, down and up, she scanned me, barely replying in monosyllables to my attempts at conversation; finally getting up, and coming nearer, and examining my clothes, and my child's still more closely. A very few minutes of this were more than I could bear; and, almost crying, I said, "Why, mamma, what makes you do so?" Then the play was over; and she was once more the wise and tender mother, telling me playfully that it was precisely in such a way I had stared, the day before, at the clothes of two ladies who had come in to visit her. I never needed that lesson again. To this day, if I find myself departing from it for an instant, the old tingling shame burns in my cheeks.

To this day, also, the old tingling pain burns my cheeks as I recall certain rude and contemptuous words which were said to me when I was very young, and stamped on my memory forever. I was once called a "stupid child" in the presence of strangers. I had brought the wrong book from my father's study. Nothing could be said to me to-day which would give me a tenth part of the hopeless sense of degradation which came from those words. Another time, on the arrival of an unexpected guest to dinner, I was sent, in a great hurry, away from the table, to make room, with the remark that "it was not of the least consequence about the child; she could just as well have her dinner afterward." "The child" would have been only too happy to help on the hospitality of the sudden emergency, if the thing had been differently put; but the sting of having it put in that way I never forgot. Yet in both these instances the rudeness was so small, in comparison with what we habitually see, that it would be too trivial to mention, except for the bearing of the fact that the pain it gave has lasted till now.

When we consider seriously what ought to be the nature of a reproof from a parent to a child, and what is its end, the answer is simple enough. It should be nothing but the superior wisdom and strength, explaining to inexperience and feebleness wherein they have made a mistake, to the end that they may avoid such mistakes in future. If personal annoyance, impatience, antagonism enter in, the relation is marred and the end endangered. Most sacred and inalienable of all rights is the right of helplessness to protection from the strong, of ignorance to counsel from the wise.

If we give our protection and counsel grudgingly, or in a churlish, unkind manner, even to the stranger that is in our gates, we are no Christians, and deserve to be stripped of what little wisdom and strength we have hoarded. But there are no words to say what we are or what we deserve if we do thus to the little children whom we have dared, for our own pleasure, to bring into the perils of this life, and whose whole future may be blighted by the mistakes of our careless hands.

BREAKING THE WILL.

THIS phrase is going out of use. It is high time it did. If the thing it represents would also cease, there would be stronger and freer men and women. But the phrase is still sometimes heard; and there are still conscientious fathers and mothers who believe they do God service in setting about the thing.

I have more than once said to a parent who used these words, "Will you tell me just what you mean by that? Of course you do not mean exactly what you say."

"Yes, I do. I mean that the child's will is to be once for all broken! — that he is to learn that my will is to be his law. The sooner he learns this the better."

"But is it to your will simply *as* will that he is to yield? Simply as the weaker yields to the stronger, — almost as matter yields to force? For what reason is he to do this?"

"Why, because I know what is best for him, and what is right; and he does not."

"Ah! that is a very different thing. He is, then, to do the thing that you tell him to do, because that thing is right and is needful for him; you are his guide on a road over which you have gone, and he has not; you are an interpreter, a helper; you know better than he does about all things, and your knowledge is to teach his ignorance."

"Certainly, that is what I mean. A pretty state of things it would be if children were to be allowed to think they know as much as their parents. There is no way except to break their wills in the beginning."

"But you have just said that it is not to your will as will that he is to yield, but to your superior knowledge and experience. That surely is not 'breaking his will.' It is of all things furthest removed from it. It is educating his will. It is teaching him how to will."

This sounds dangerous; but the logic is not easily turned aside, and there is little left for the advocate of will-breaking but to fall back on some texts in the Bible, which have been so often misquoted in this connection that one can hardly hear them with patience. To "Children, obey your parents," was added "in the Lord," and "because it is right," not "because they are your parents." "Spare the rod" has been quite gratuitously assumed to mean "spare blows." "Rod" means here, as elsewhere, simply punishment. We are not told to "train up a child" to have no will but our own, but "in the way in which he should go," and to the end that "when he is old" he should not "depart from it," — *i. e.*, that his will should be so educated that he will choose to walk in the right way still. Suppose a child's will to be actually "broken;" suppose him to be so trained that he has no will but to obey his parents. What is to become of this helpless machine, which has no central spring of independent action? Can we stand by, each minute of each hour of each day, and say to the automata, Go here, or Go there? Can we be sure of living as long as they live? Can we wind them up like seventy-year clocks, and leave them?

But this is idle. It is not, thank God, in the power of any man or any woman to "break" a child's "will." They may kill the child's body, in trying, like that still unhung clergyman in Western New York, who whipped his three-year-old son to death for refusing to repeat a prayer to his step-mother.

Bodies are frail things; there are more child-martyrs than will be known until the bodies terrestrial are done with.

But, by one escape or another, the will, the soul, goes free. Sooner or later, every human being comes to know and prove in his own estate that freedom of will is the only freedom for which there are no chains possible, and that in Nature's whole reign of law nothing is so largely provided for as liberty. Sooner or later, all this must come. But, if it comes later, it comes through clouds of antagonism, and after days of fight, and is hard-bought.

It should come sooner, like the kingdom of God, which it is, — "without observation," gracious as sunshine, sweet as dew; it should begin with the infant's first dawning of comprehension that there are two courses of action, two qualities of conduct: one wise, the other foolish; one right, the other wrong.

I am sure; for I have seen, that a child's moral perceptions can be so made clear, and his will so made strong and upright, that before he is ten years old he will see and take his way through all common days rightly and bravely.

Will he always act up to his highest moral perceptions? No. Do we? But one right decision that he makes voluntarily, unbiassed by the assertion of authority or the threat of punishment, is worth more to him in development of moral character than a thousand in which he simply does what he is compelled to do by some sort of outside pressure.

I read once, in a book intended for the guidance of mothers, a story of a little child who, in repeating his letters one day, suddenly refused to say A. All the other letters he repeated again and again, unhesitatingly; but A he would not, and persisted in declaring that he could not say. He was severely whipped, but still persisted. It now became a contest of wills. He was whipped again and again and again. In the intervals between the whippings the primer was presented to him, and he was told that he would be whipped again if he did not mind his mother and say A. I forget how many times he was whipped; but it was almost too many times to be believed. The fight was a terrible one. At last, in a paroxysm of his crying under the blows, the mother thought she heard him sob out "A," and the victory was considered to be won.

A little boy whom I know once had a similar contest over a letter of the alphabet; but the contest was with himself, and his mother was the faithful Great Heart who helped him through. The story is so remarkable that I have long wanted all mothers to know it. It is as perfect an illustration of what I mean by "educating" the will as the other one is of what is called "breaking" it.

Willy was about four years old. He had a large, active brain, sensitive temperament, and indomitable spirit. He was and is an uncommon child. Common methods of what is commonly supposed to be "discipline" would, if he had survived them, have made a very bad boy of him. He had great difficulty in pronouncing the letter G, — so much that he had formed almost a habit of omitting it. One day his mother said, not dreaming of any special contest, "This time you must say G." "It is an ugly old letter, and I ain't ever going to try to say it again," said Willy, repeating the alphabet very rapidly from beginning to end, without the G. Like a wise mother, she did not open at once on a struggle; but said, pleasantly, "Ah! you did not get it in that time. Try again; go more slowly, and we will have it." It was all in vain; and it soon began to look more like real obstinacy on Willy's part than any thing she had ever seen in him. She has often told me how she hesitated before entering on the campaign. "I always knew," she said, "that Willy's first real fight with himself would be no matter of a few hours; and it was a particularly inconvenient time for me, just then, to give up a day to it. But it seemed, on the whole, best not to put it off."

So she said, "Now, Willy, you can't get along without the letter G. The longer you put off saying it, the harder it will be for you to say it at last; and we will have it settled now, once for all. You are never going to let a little bit of a letter like that be stronger than Willy. We will not go out of this room till you have said it."

Unfortunately, Willy's will had already taken its stand. However, the mother made no authoritative demand that he should pronounce the letter as a matter of obedience to her. Because it was a thing intrinsically necessary for him to do, she would see, at any cost to herself or to him, that he did it; but he must do it voluntarily, and she would wait till he did.

The morning wore on. She busied herself with other matters, and left Willy to himself; now and then asking, with a smile, "Well, isn't my little boy stronger than that ugly old letter yet?"

Willy was sulky. He understood in that early stage all that was involved. Dinner-time came.

"Aren't you going to dinner, mamma?"

"Oh! no, dear; not unless you say G, so that you can go too. Mamma will stay by her little boy until he is out of this trouble."

The dinner was brought up, and they ate it together. She was cheerful and kind, but so serious that he felt the constant pressure of her pain.

The afternoon dragged slowly on to night. Willy cried now and then, and she took him in her lap, and said, "Dear, you will be happy as soon as you say that letter, and mamma will be happy too, and we can't either of us be happy until you do."

"Oh, mamma! why don't you *make* me say it?"

(This he said several times before the affair was over.)

"Because, dear, you must make yourself say it. I am helping you make yourself say it, for I shall not let you go out of this room, nor go out myself, till you do say it; but that is all I shall do to help you. I am listening, listening all the time, and if you say it, in ever so little a whisper, I shall hear you. That is all mamma can do for you."

Bed-time came. Willy went to bed, unkissed and sad. The next morning, when Willy's mother opened her eyes, she saw Willy sitting up in his crib, and looking at her steadfastly. As soon as he saw that she was awake, he exclaimed, "Mamma, I can't say it; and you know I can't say it. You're a naughty mamma, and you don't love me." Her heart sank within her; but she patiently went again and again over yesterday's ground. Willy cried. He ate very little breakfast. He stood at the window in a listless attitude of discouraged misery, which she said cut her to the heart. Once in a while he would ask for some plaything which he did not usually have. She gave him whatever he asked for; but he could not play. She kept up an appearance of being busy with her sewing, but she was far more unhappy than Willy.

Dinner was brought up to them. Willy said, "Mamma, this ain't a bit good dinner."

She replied, "Yes, it is, darling; just as good as we ever have. It is only because we are eating it alone. And poor papa is sad, too, taking his all alone downstairs."

At this Willy burst out into an hysterical fit of crying and sobbing.

"I shall never see my papa again in this world."

Then his mother broke down, too, and cried as hard as he did; but she said, "Oh! yes, you will, dear. I think you will say that lĕtter before tea-time, and we will have a nice evening downstairs together."

"I can't say it. I try all the time, and I can't say it; and, if you keep me here till I die, I shan't ever say it."

The second night settled down dark and gloomy, and Willy cried himself to sleep. His mother was ill from anxiety and confinement; but she never faltered. She told me she resolved that night that, if it were necessary, she would stay in that room with Willy a month. The next morning she said to him, more seriously than before, "Now, Willy, you are not only a foolish little boy, you are unkind; you are making everybody unhappy. Mamma is very sorry for you, but she is also very much displeased with you. Mamma will stay here with you till you say that letter, if it is for the rest of your life; but mamma will not talk with you, as she did yesterday. She tried all day yesterday to help you, and you would not help yourself; to-day you must do it all alone."

"Mamma, are you sure I shall ever say it?" asked Willy.

"Yes, dear; perfectly sure. You will say it some day or other,"

"Do you think I shall say it to-day?"

"I can't tell. You are not so strong a little boy as I thought. I believed you would say it yesterday. I am afraid you have some hard work before you."

Willy begged her to go down and leave him alone. Then he begged her to shut him up in the closet, and "see if that wouldn't make him good." Every few minutes he would come and stand before her, and say very earnestly, "Are you sure I shall say it?"

He looked very pale, almost as if he had had a fit of illness. No wonder. It was the whole battle of life fought at the age of four.

It was late in the afternoon of this the third day. Willy had been sitting in his little chair, looking steadily at the floor, for so long a time that his mother was almost frightened. But she hesitated to speak to him, for she felt that the crisis had come. Suddenly he sprang up, and walked toward her with all the deliberate firmness of a man in his whole bearing. She says there was something in his face which she has never seen since, and does not expect to see till he is thirty years old.

"Mamma!" said he.

"Well, dear?" said his mother, trembling so that she could hardly speak.

"Mamma," he repeated, in a loud, sharp tone, "G! G! G! G!" And then he burst into a fit of crying, which she had hard work to stop. It was over.

Willy is now ten years old. From that day to this his mother has never had a contest with him; she has always been able to leave all practical questions affecting his behavior to his own decision, merely saying, "Willy, I think this or that will be better."

His self-control and gentleness are wonderful to see; and the blending in his face of childlike simplicity and purity with manly strength is something which I have only once seen equalled.

For a few days he went about the house, shouting "G! G! G!" at the top of his voice. He was heard asking playmates if they could "say G," and "who showed them how." For several years he used often to allude to the affair, saying, "Do you remember, mamma, that dreadful time when I wouldn't say G?" He always used the verb "wouldn't" in speaking of it. Once, when he was sick, he said, "Mamma, do you think I could have said G any sooner than I did?"

"I have never felt certain about that, Willy," she said. "What do *you* think?"

"I think I could have said it a few minutes sooner. I was saying it to *myself* as long as that!" said Willy.

It was singular that, although up to that time he had never been able to pronounce the letter with any distinctness, when he first made up his mind in this instance to say it, he enunciated it with perfect clearness, and never again went back to the old, imperfect pronunciation.

Few mothers, perhaps, would be able to give up two whole days to such a battle as this; other children, other duties, would interfere. But the same principle could be carried out without the mother's remaining herself by the child's side all the time. Moreover, not one child in a thousand would hold out as Willy did. In all ordinary cases a few hours would suffice. And, after all, what would the sacrifice of even two days be, in comparison with the time saved in years to come? If there were no stronger motive than one of policy, of desire to take the course easiest to themselves, mothers might well resolve that their first aim should be to educate their children's wills and make them strong, instead of to conquer and "break" them.

THE REIGN OF ARCHELAUS.

HEROD'S massacre had, after all, a certain mercy in it: there were no lingering tortures. The slayers of children went about with naked and bloody swords, which mothers could see, and might at least make effort to flee from. Into Rachel's refusal to be comforted there need enter no bitter agonies of remorse. But Herod's death, it seems, did not make Judea a safe place for babies. When Joseph "heard that Archelaus did reign in the room of his father, Herod, he was afraid to return thither with the infant Jesus," and only after repeated commands and warnings from God would he venture as far as Nazareth. The reign of Archelaus is not yet over; he has had many names, and ruled over more and more countries, but the spirit of his father, Herod, is still in him. To-day his power is at its zenith. He is called Education; and the safest place for the dear, holy children is still Egypt, or some other of the fortunate countries called unenlightened.

Some years ago there were symptoms of a strong rebellion against his tyranny. Horace Mann lifted up his strong hands and voice against it; physicians and physiologists came out gravely and earnestly, and fortified their positions with statistics from which there was no appeal. Thomas Wentworth Higginson, whose words have with the light, graceful beauty of the Damascus blade its swift sureness in cleaving to the heart of things, wrote an article for the "Atlantic Monthly" called "The Murder of the Innocents," which we wish could be put into every house in the United States. Some changes in school organizations resulted from these protests; in the matter of ventilation of schoolrooms some real improvement was probably effected; though we shudder to think how much room remains for further improvement, when we read in the report of the superintendent of public schools in Brooklyn that in the primary departments of the grammar schools "an average daily number of 33,275 pupils are crowded into one-half the space provided in the upper departments for an average daily attendance of 26,359; or compelled to occupy badly lighted, inconvenient, and ill-ventilated galleries, or rooms in the basement stories."

But in regard to the number of hours of confinement, and amount of study required of children, it is hard to believe that schools have ever been much more murderously exacting than now.

The substitution of the single session of five hours for the old arrangement of two sessions of three hours each, with a two-hours interval at noon, was regarded as a great gain. So it would be, if all the brain-work of the day were done in that time; but in most schools with the five-hours session, there is next to no provision for studying in school-hours, and the pupils are required to learn two, three, or four lessons at home. Now, when is your boy to learn these lessons? Not in the morning, before school; that is plain. School ends at two. Few children live sufficiently near their schools to get home to dinner before half past two o'clock. We say nothing of the undesirableness of taking the hearty meal of the day immediately after five hours of mental fatigue; it is probably a less evil than the late dinner at six, and we are in a region where we are grateful for *less* evils! Dinner is over at quarter past three; we make close estimates. In winter there is left less than two hours before dark. This is all the time the child is to have for out-door play; two hours and a half (counting in his recess) out of twenty-four. Ask any farmer, even the stupidest, how well his colt or his lamb would grow if it had but two hours a day of absolute freedom and exercise in the open air, and that in the dark and the chill of a late afternoon! In spite of the dark and the chill, however, your boy skates or slides on until he is called in by you, who, if you are an American mother, care a great deal more than he does for the bad marks which will stand on his week's report if those three lessons are not learned before bed-time. He is tired and cold; he does not want to study —who would? It is six o'clock before he is fairly at it. You work harder than he does, and in half an hour one lesson is learned; then comes tea. After tea half an hour, or perhaps an hour, remains before bed-time; in this time, which ought to be spent in light, cheerful talk or play, the rest of the lessons must be learned. He is sleepy and discouraged. Words which in the freshness of the morning he would have learned in a very few moments with ease, it is now simply out of his power to commit to memory. You, if you are not superhuman, grow impatient. At eight o'clock he goes to bed, his brain excited and wearied, in no condition for healthful sleep; and his heart oppressed with the fear of "missing" in the next day's recitations. And this is one out of the school-year's two hundred and sixteen days — all of which will be like this, or worse. One of the most pitiful sights we have seen for months was a little group of four dear children, gathered round the library lamp, trying to learn the next day's lessons in time to have a story read to them before going to bed. They had taken the precaution to learn one lesson immediately after dinner, before going out, cutting their out-door play down by half an hour. The two elder were learning a long spelling-lesson; the third was grappling with geographical definitions of capes, promontories, and so forth; and the youngest was at work on his primer. In spite of all their efforts, bed-time came before the lessons were learned. The little geography student had been nodding over her book for some minutes, and she had the philosophy to say, "I don't care; I'm so sleepy. I had rather go to bed than hear any kind of a story." But the elder ones were grieved and unhappy, and said, "There won't *ever* be any time; we shall have just as much more to learn to-morrow night." The next morning, however, there was a sight still more pitiful: the baby of seven, with a little bit of paper and a pencil, and three sums in addition to be done, and the father vainly endeavoring to explain them to him in the hurried moments before breakfast. It would be easy to show how fatal to all real mental development, how false to all Nature's laws of growth, such a system must be; but that belongs to another side of the question. We speak now simply of the effect of it on the body; and here we quote largely from the admirable article of Col. Higginson's, above referred to. No stronger, more direct, more conclusive words can be written: —

"Sir Walter Scott, according to Carlyle, was the only perfectly healthy literary man who ever lived. He gave it as his deliberate opinion, in conversation with Basil Hall, that five and a half hours form the limit of healthful mental labor for a mature person. 'This I reckon very good work for a man,' he said. 'I can very seldom work six hours a day.' Supposing his estimate to be correct, and five and a half hours the reasonable limit for the day's work of a mature intellect, it is evident that even this must be altogether too much for an immature one. 'To suppose the youthful brain,' says the recent admirable report, by Dr. Ray, of the Providence Insane Hospital, 'to be capable of an amount of work which is considered an ample allowance to an adult brain is simply absurd.' 'It would be wrong, therefore, to deduct less than a halfhoür from Scott's estimate, for even the oldest pupils in our highest schools, leaving five hours as the limit of real mental effort for them, and reducing this for all younger pupils very much further.'

"But Scott is not the only authority in the case; let us ask the physiologists. So said Horace Mann before us, in the days when the Massachusetts school system was in process of formation. He asked the physicians in 1840, and in his report printed the answers of three of the most eminent. The late Dr. Woodward, of Worcester, promptly said that children under eight should never be confined more than one hour at a time, nor more than four hours a day.

"Dr. James Jackson, of Boston, allowed the children four hours schooling in winter and five in summer, but only one hour at a time; and heartily expressed his detestation of giving young children lessons to learn at home.

"Dr. S. G. Howe, reasoning elaborately on the whole subject, said that children under eight years of age should never be confined more than half an hour at a time; by following which rule, with long recesses, they can study four hours daily. Children between eight and fourteen should not be confined more than three-quarters of an hour at a time, having the last quarter of each hour for exercise on the playground.

"Indeed, the one thing about which doctors do *not* disagree is the destructive effect of premature or excessive mental labor. I can quote you medical authority for and against every maxim of dietetics beyond the very simplest; but I defy you to find one man who ever begged, borrowed, or stole the title of M.D., and yet abused those two honorary letters by asserting under their cover that a child could safely study as much as a man, or that a man could safely study more than six hours a day."

"The worst danger of it is that the moral is written at the end of the fable, not at the beginning. The organization in youth is so dangerously elastic that the result of these intellectual excesses is not seen until years after. When some young girl incurs spinal disease from some slight fall, which she ought not to have felt for an hour, or some business man breaks down in the prime of his years from some trifling over-anxiety, which should have left no trace behind, the popular verdict may be 'Mysterious Providence;' but the wiser observer sees the retribution for the folly of those misspent days which enfeebled the childish constitution instead of ripening it. One of the most striking passages in the report of Dr. Ray, before mentioned, is that in which he explains that, 'though study at school is rarely the immediate cause of insanity, it is the most frequent of its ulterior causes, except hereditary tendencies.' *It diminishes the conservative power of the animal economy to such a degree that attacks of disease which otherwise would have passed off safely destroy life almost before danger is anticipated.*"

It would be easy to multiply authorities on these points. It is hard to stop. But our limits forbid any thing like a full treatment of the subject. Yet discussion on this question ought never to cease in the land until a reform is brought about. Teachers are to blame only in part for the present wrong state of things. They are to blame for yielding, for acquiescing; but the real blame rests on parents. Here and there, individual fathers and mothers, taught, perhaps, by heart-rending experience, try to make stand against the current of false ambitions and unhealthy standards. But these are rare exceptions. Parents, as a class, not only help on, but create the pressure to which teachers yield, and children are sacrificed. The whole responsibility is really theirs. They have in their hands the power to regulate the whole school routine to which their children are to be subjected. This is plain, when we once consider what would be the immediate effect in any community, large or small, if a majority of parents took action together, and persistently refused to allow any child under fourteen to be confined in school more than four hours out of the twenty-four, more than one hour at a time, or to do more than five hours' brain-work in a day. The law of supply and demand is a first principle. In three months the schools in that community would be entirely reorganized, to accord with the parents' wishes; in three years the improved average health of the children in that community would bear its own witness in ruddy bloom along the streets; and perhaps even in one generation so great gain of vigor might be made that the melancholy statistics of burial would no longer have to record the death under twelve years of age of more than two-fifths of the children who are born.

THE AWKWARD AGE.

THE expression defines itself. At the first sound of the words, we all think of some one unhappy soul we know just now, whom they suggest. Nobody is ever without at least one brother, sister, cousin, or friend on hand, who is struggling through this social slough of despond; and nobody ever will be, so long as the world goes on taking it for granted that the slough is a necessity, and that the road must go through it. Nature never meant any such thing. Now and then she blunders or gets thwarted of her intent, and turns out a person who is awkward, hopelessly and forever awkward; body and soul are clumsy together, and it is hard to fancy them translated to the spiritual world without too much elbow and ankle. However, these are rare cases, and come in under the law of variation. But an awkward age, — a necessary crisis or stage of uncouthness, through which all human beings must pass, — Nature was incapable of such a conception; law has no place for it; development does not know it; instinct revolts from it; and man is the only animal who has been silly and wrong-headed enough to stumble into it. The explanation and the remedy are so simple, so close at hand, that we have not seen them. The whole thing lies in a nutshell. Where does this abnormal, uncomfortable period come in? Between childhood, we say, and maturity; it is the transition from one to the other. When human beings, then, are neither boys nor men, girls nor women, they must be for a few years anomalous creatures, must they? We might, perhaps, find a name for the individual in this condition as well as for the condition. We must look to Du Chaillu for it, if we do; but it is too serious a distress to make light of, even for a moment. We have all felt it, and we know how it feels; we all see it every day, and we know how it looks.

What is it which the child has and the adult loses, from the loss of which comes this total change of behavior? Or is it something which the adult has and the child had not? It is both; and until the loss and the gain, the new and the old, are permanently separated and balanced, the awkward age lasts. The child was overlooked, contradicted, thwarted, snubbed, insulted, whipped; not constantly, not often, — in many cases, thank God, very seldom. But the liability was there, and he knew it; he never forgot it, if you did. One burn is enough to make fire dreaded. The adult, once fairly recognized as adult, is not overlooked, contradicted, thwarted, snubbed, insulted, whipped; at least, not with impunity. To this gratifying freedom, these comfortable exemptions, when they are once established in our belief, we adjust ourselves, and grow contentedly good-mannered. To the other *régime*, while we were yet children, we also somewhat adjusted ourselves, were tolerably well behaved, and made the best of it. But who could bear a mixture of both? What genius could rise superior to it, could be itself, surrounded by such uncertainties?

No wonder that your son comes into the room with a confused expression of uncomfortable pain on every feature, when he does not in the least know whether he will be recognized as a gentleman, or overlooked as a little boy. No wonder he sits down in his chair with movements suggestive of nothing but rheumatism and jack-knives, when he is thinking that perhaps there may be some reason why he should not take that particular chair, and that, if there is, he will be ordered up.

No wonder that your tall daughter turns red, stammers, and says foolish things on being courteously spoken to by strangers at dinner, when she is afraid that she may be sharply contradicted or interrupted, and remembers that day before yesterday she was told that children should be seen and not heard.

I knew a very clever girl, who had the misfortune to look at fourteen as if she were twenty. At home, she was the shyest and most awkward of creatures; away from her mother and sisters, she was self-possessed and charming. She said to me, once, "Oh! I have such a splendid time away from home. I'm so tall, everybody thinks I am grown up, and everybody is civil to me."

I know, also, a man of superb physique, charming temperament, and uncommon talent, who is to this day — and he is twenty-five years old — nervous and ill at ease in talking with strangers, in the presence of his own family. He hesitates, stammers, and never does justice to his thoughts. He says that he believes he shall never be free from this distress ; he cannot escape from the recollections of the years between fourteen and twenty, during which he was so systematically snubbed that his mother's parlor was to him worse than the chambers of the Inquisition. He knows that he is now sure of courteous treatment ; that his friends are all proud of him ; but the old cloud will never entirely disappear. Something has been lost which can never be regained. And the loss is not his alone, it is theirs too ; they are all poorer for life, by reason of the unkind days which are gone.

This, then, is the explanation of the awkward age. I am not afraid of any dissent from my definition of the source whence its misery springs. Everybody's consciousness bears witness. Everybody knows, in the bottom of his heart, that, however much may be said about the change of voice, the thinness of cheeks, the sharpness of arms, the sudden length in legs and lack of length in trousers and frocks, — all these had nothing to do with the real misery. The real misery was simply and solely the horrible feeling of not belonging anywhere ; not knowing what a moment might bring forth in the way of treatment from others ; never being sure which impulse it would be safer to follow, to retreat or to advance, to speak or to be silent, and often overwhelmed with unspeakable mortification at the rebuff of the one or the censure of the other. Oh ! how dreadful it all was! How dreadful it all is, even to remember! It would be malicious even to refer to it, except to point out the cure.

The cure is plain. It needs no experiment to test it. Merely to mention it ought to be enough. If human beings are so awkward at this unhappy age, and so unhappy at this awkward age, simply because they do not know whether they are to be treated as children or as adults, suppose we make a rule that children are always to be treated, in point of courtesy, as if they were adults? Then this awkward age — this period of transition from an atmosphere of, to say the least, negative rudeness to one of gracious politeness — disappears. There cannot be a crisis of readjustment of social relations: there is no possibility of such a feeling; it would be hard to explain to a young person what it meant. Now and then we see a young man or young woman who has never known it. They are usually only children, and are commonly spoken of as wonders. I know such a boy to-day. At seventeen he measures six feet in height; he has the feet and the hands of a still larger man; and he comes of a blood which had far more strength than grace. But his manner is, and always has been, sweet, gentle, composed, — the very ideal of grave, tender, frank young manhood. People say, "How strange! He never seemed to have any awkward age at all." It would have been stranger if he had. Neither his father nor his mother ever departed for an instant, in their relations with him, from the laws of courtesy and kindliness of demeanor which governed their relations with others.

He knew but one atmosphere, and that a genial one, from his babyhood up; and in and of this atmosphere has grown up a sweet, strong, pure soul, for which the quiet, self-possessed manner is but the fitting garb.

This is part of the kingdom that cometh unobserved. In this kingdom we are all to be kings and priests, if we choose; and all its ways are pleasantness. But we are not ready for it till we have become peaceable and easy to be entreated, and have learned to understand why it was that one day, when Jesus called his disciples together, he set a little child in their midst.

A DAY WITH A COURTEOUS MOTHER.

DURING the whole of one of last summer's hottest days I had the good fortune to be seated in a railway car near a mother and four children, whose relations with each other were so beautiful that the pleasure of watching them was quite enough to make one forget the discomforts of the journey.

It was plain that they were poor; their clothes were coarse and old, and had been made by inexperienced hands. The mother's bonnet alone would have been enough to have condemned the whole party on any of the world's thoroughfares. I remembered afterward, with shame, that I myself had smiled at the first sight of its antiquated ugliness; but her face was one which it gave you a sense of rest to look upon, — it was so earnest, tender, true, and strong. It had little comeliness of shape or color in it, it was thin, and pale; she was not young; she had worked hard; she had evidently been much ill; but I have seen few faces which gave me such pleasure. I think that she was the wife of a poor clergyman; and I think that clergyman must be one of the Lord's best watchmen of souls. The children — two boys and two girls —

were all under the age of twelve, and the youngest could not speak plainly. They had had a rare treat; they had been visiting the mountains, and they were talking over all the wonders they had seen with a glow of enthusiastic delight which was to be envied. Only a word-for-word record would do justice to their conversation; no description could give any idea of it, — so free, so pleasant, so genial, no interruptions, no contradictions; and the mother's part borne all the while with such equal interest and eagerness that no one not seeing her face would dream that she was any other than an elder sister. In the course of the day there were many occasions when it was necessary for her to deny requests, and to ask services, especially from the eldest boy; but no young girl, anxious to please a lover, could have done either with a more tender courtesy. She had her reward; for no lover could have been more tender and manly than was this boy of twelve. Their lunch was simple and scanty; but it had the grace of a royal banquet. At the last, the mother produced with much glee three apples and an orange, of which the children had not known. All eyes fastened on the orange. It was evidently a great rarity. I watched to see if this test would bring out selfishness. There was a little silence; just the shade of a cloud. The mother said, "How shall I divide this? There is one for each of you; and I shall be best off of all, for I expect big tastes from each of you."

"Oh, give Annie the orange. Annie loves oranges,"

spoke out the oldest boy, with a sudden air of a conqueror, and at the same time taking the smallest and worst apple himself.

"Oh, yes, let Annie have the orange," echoed the second boy, nine years old.

"Yes, Annie may have the orange, because that is nicer than the apple, and she is a lady, and her brothers are gentlemen," said the mother, quietly. Then there was a merry contest as to who should feed the mother with largest and most frequent mouthfuls; and so the feast went on. Then Annie pretended to want apple, and exchanged thin golden strips of orange for bites out of the cheeks of Baldwins; and, as I sat watching her intently, she suddenly fancied she saw longing in my face, and sprang over to me, holding out a quarter of her orange, and saying, "Don't you want a taste, too?" The mother smiled, understandingly, when I said, "No, I thank you, you dear, generous little girl; I don't care about oranges."

At noon we had a tedious interval of waiting at a dreary station. We sat for two hours on a narrow platform, which the sun had scorched till it smelt of heat. The oldest boy — the little lover — held the youngest child, and talked to her, while the tired mother closed her eyes and rested. Now and then he looked over at her, and then back at the baby; and at last he said confidentially to me (for we had become fast friends by this time), "Isn't it funny, to think that I was ever so small as this baby? And papa says that then mamma was almost a little girl herself."

The two other children were toiling up and down the banks of the railroad-track, picking ox-eye daisies, buttercups, and sorrel. They worked like beavers, and soon the bunches were almost too big for their little hands. Then they came running to give them to their mother. "Oh dear," thought I, "how that poor, tired woman will hate to open her eyes! and she never can take those great bunches of common, fading flowers, in addition to all her bundles and bags." I was mistaken.

"Oh, thank you, my darlings! How kind you were! Poor, hot, tired little flowers, how thirsty they look! If they will only try and keep alive till we get home, we will make them very happy in some water; won't we? And you shall put one bunch by papa's plate, and one by mine."

Sweet and happy, the weary and flushed little children stood looking up in her face while she talked, their hearts thrilling with compassion for the drooping flowers and with delight in the giving of their gift. Then she took great trouble to get a string and tie up the flowers, and then the train came, and we were whirling along again. Soon it grew dark, and little Annie's head nodded. Then I heard the mother say to the oldest boy, "Dear, are you too tired to let little Annie put her head on your shoulder and take a nap? We shall get her home in much better case to see papa if we can manage to give her a little sleep." How many boys of twelve hear such words as these from tired, overburdened mothers?

Soon came the city, the final station, with its bustle and noise. I lingered to watch my happy family, hoping to see the father. "Why, papa isn't here!" exclaimed one disappointed little voice after another. "Never mind," said the mother, with a still deeper disappointment in her own tone; "perhaps he had to go to see some poor body who is sick." In the hurry of picking up all the parcels, and the sleepy babies, the poor daisies and buttercups were left forgotten in a corner of the rack. I wondered if the mother had not intended this. May I be forgiven for the injustice! A few minutes after I passed the little group, standing still just outside the station, and heard the mother say, "Oh, my darlings, I have forgotten your pretty bouquets. I am so sorry! I wonder if I could find them if I went back. Will you all stand still and not stir from this spot if I go?"

"Oh, mamma, don't go, don't go. We will get you some more. Don't go," cried all the children.

"Here are your flowers, madam," said I. "I saw that you had forgotten them, and I took them as mementoes of you and your sweet children." She blushed and looked disconcerted. She was evidently unused to people, and shy with all but her children. However, she thanked me sweetly, and said, —

"I was very sorry about them. The children took such trouble to get them; and I think they will revive in water. They cannot be quite dead."

"They will *never* die!" said I, with an emphasis which went from my heart to hers. Then all her shyness fled. She knew me; and we shook hands, and smiled into each other's eyes with the smile of kindred as we parted.

As I followed on, I heard the two children, who were walking behind, saying to each other, "Wouldn't that have been too bad? Mamma liked them so much, and we never could have got so many all at once again."

"Yes, we could, too, next summer," said the boy, sturdily.

They are sure of their "next summers," I think, all six of those souls, — children, and mother, and father. They may never again gather so many ox-eye daisies and buttercups "all at once." Perhaps some of the little hands have already picked their last flowers. Nevertheless, their summers are certain. To such souls as these, all trees, either here or in God's larger country, are Trees of Life, with twelve manner of fruits and leaves for healing; and it is but little change from the summers here, whose suns burn and make weary, to the summers there, of which "the Lamb is the light."

Heaven bless them all, wherever they are.

CHILDREN IN NOVA SCOTIA.

NOVA SCOTIA is a country of gracious surprises. Instead of the stones which are what strangers chiefly expect at her hands, she gives us a wealth of fertile meadows ; instead of stormy waves breaking on a frowning coast, she shows us smooth basins whose shores are soft and wooded to the water's edge, and into which empty wonderful tidal rivers, whose courses, where the tide-water has flowed out, lie like curving bands of bright brown satin among the green fields. She has no barrenness, no unsightliness, no poverty; everywhere beauty, everywhere riches. She is biding her time.

But most beautiful among her beauties, most wonderful among her wonders, are her children. During two weeks' travel in the provinces, I have been constantly more and more impressed by their superiority in appearance, size, and health to the children of the New England and Middle States. In the outset of our journey I was struck by it ; along all the roadsides they looked up, boys and girls, fair, broad-cheeked, sturdy-legged, such as with us are seen only now and then. I did not, however, realize at first that this was the universal law of the land, and that it pointed to something more than climate as a cause. But the first school that I saw, *en masse*, gave a startling impetus to the train of observation and inference into which I was unconsciously falling. It was a Sunday school in the little town of Wolfville, which lies between the Gaspcreau and Cornwallis rivers, just beyond the meadows of the Grand Pré, where lived Gabriel Lajeunesse, and Benedict Bellefontaine, and the rest of the "simple Acadian farmers."

"Mists from the mighty Atlantic" more than "looked on the happy valley" that Sunday morning. Convicting Longfellow of a mistake, they did descend "from their stations," on solemn Blomidon, and fell in a slow, unpleasant drizzle in the streets of Wolfville and Horton. I arrived too early at one of the village churches, and while I was waiting for a sexton a door opened, and out poured the Sunday school, whose services had just ended. On they came, dividing in the centre, and falling to the right and left about me, thirty or forty boys and girls, between the ages of seven and fifteen. I looked at them in astonishment. They all had fair skins, red cheeks, and clear eyes; they were all broad-shouldered, straight, and sturdy; the younger ones were more than sturdy,— they were fat, from the ankles up. But perhaps the most noticeable thing of all was the quiet, sturdy, unharassed expression which their faces wore; a look which is the greatest charm of a child's face, but which we rarely see in children over two or three years old. Boys of eleven or twelve were there, with shoulders broader than the average of our boys at sixteen, and yet with the pure, childlike look on their faces. Girls of ten or eleven were there who looked almost like women, — that is, like ideal women, — simply because they looked so calm and undisturbed. The Saxon coloring prevailed; three-fourths of the eyes were blue, with hair of that pale ash-brown which the French call "*blonde cendrée.*" Out of them all there was but one child who looked sickly. He had evidently met with some accident, and was lame. Afterward, as the congregation assembled, I watched the fathers and mothers of these children. They, too, were broad-shouldered, tall, and straight, especially the women. Even old women were straight, like the negroes one sees at the South, walking with burdens on their heads.

Five days later I saw in Halifax the celebration of the anniversary of the settlement of the province. The children of the city and of some of the neighboring towns marched in "bands of hope" and processions, such as we see in the cities of the States on the Fourth of July. This was just the opportunity I wanted. It was the same here as in the country. I counted on that day just eleven sickly-looking children; no more! Such brilliant cheeks, such merry eyes, such evident strength; it was a scene to kindle the dullest soul. There were scores of little ones there, whose droll, fat legs would have drawn a crowd in Central Park; and they all had that same, quiet, composed, well-balanced expression of countenance of which I spoke before, and of which it would be hard to find an instance in all Central Park.

Climate undoubtedly has something to do with this. The air is moist, and the mercury rarely rises above 80° or falls below 10°. Also the comparative quiet of their lives helps to make them so beautiful and strong. But the most significant fact to my mind is that, until the past year, there have been in Nova Scotia no public schools, comparatively few private ones; and in these there is no severe pressure brought to bear on the pupils. The private schools have been expensive, consequently it has been very unusual for children to be sent to school before they were *eight or nine* years of age; I could not find a person who had ever known of a child's being sent to school *under seven!* The school sessions are on the old plan of six hours per day, — from nine till twelve, and from one till four; but no learning of lessons out of school has been allowed. Within the last year a system of free public schools has been introduced, "and the people are grumbling terribly about it," said my informant. "Why?" I asked; "because they do not wish to have their children educated?" "Oh, no," said he; "because they do not like to pay the taxes!" "Alas!" I thought, "if it were only their silver which would be taxed!"

I must not be understood to argue from the health of the children of Nova Scotia, as contrasted with the lack of health among our children, that it is best to have no public schools; only that it is better to have no public schools than to have such public schools as are now killing off our children.

The registration system of Nova Scotia is as yet

imperfectly carried out. It is almost impossible to obtain exact returns from all parts of so thinly settled a country. But such statistics as have been already established give sufficient food for reflection in this connection. In Massachusetts more than two-fifths of all the children born die before they are twelve years old. In Nova Scotia the proportion is less than one-third. In Nova Scotia one out of every fifty-six lives to be over ninety years of age; and one-twelfth of the entire number of deaths is between the ages of eighty and ninety. In Massachusetts one person out of one hundred and nine lives to be over ninety.

In Massachusetts the mortality from diseases of the brain and nervous system is eleven per cent. In Nova Scotia it is only eight per cent.

THE REPUBLIC OF THE FAMILY.

"HE is lover and friend and son, all in one," said a friend, the other day, telling me of a dear boy who, out of his first earnings, had just sent to his mother a beautiful gift, costing much more than he could really afford for such a purpose.

That mother is the wisest, sweetest, most triumphant mother I have ever known. I am restrained by feelings of deepest reverence for her from speaking, as I might speak, of the rare and tender methods by which her motherhood has worked, patiently and alone, for nearly twenty years, and made of her two sons "lovers and friends." I have always felt that she owed it to the world to impart to other mothers all that she could of her divine secret; to write out, even in detail, all the processes by which her boys have grown to be so strong, upright, loving, and manly.

But one of her first principles has so direct a bearing on the subject that I wish to speak of here that I venture to attempt an explanation of it. She has told me that she never once, even in their childish days, took the ground that she had right to require any thing from them simply *because* she was their mother. This is a position very startling to the average parent. It is exactly counter to traditions.

"Why must I?" or "Why cannot I?" says the child. "Because I say so, and I am your father," has been the stern, authoritative reply ever since we can any of us remember; and, I presume, ever since the Christian era, since that good Apostle Paul saw enough in the Ephesian families where he visited to lead him to write to them from Rome, "Fathers, provoke not your children to wrath."

It seems to me that there are few questions of practical moment in every-day living on which a foregone and erroneous conclusion has been adopted so generally and so undoubtingly. How it first came about it is hard to see. Or, rather, it is easy to see, when one reflects; and the very clearness of the surface explanation of it only makes its injustice more odious. It came about because the parent was strong and the child weak. Helplessness in the hands of power,— that is the whole story. Suppose for an instant (and, absurd as the supposition is practically, it is not logically absurd), that the child at six were strong enough to whip his father; let him have the intellect of an infant, the mistakes and the faults of an infant,—which the father would feel himself bound and *would be* bound to correct,—but the body of a man; and then see in how different fashion the father would set himself to work to insure good behavior. I never see the heavy, impatient hand of a grown man or woman laid with its brute force, even for the smallest purpose, on a little child, without longing for a sudden miracle to give the baby an equal strength to resist.

When we realize what it is for us to dare, for our own pleasure, even with solemnest purpose of the holiest of pleasures, parenthood, to bring into existence a soul, which must take for our sake its chance of joy or sorrow, how monstrous it seems to assume that the fact that we have done this thing gives us arbitrary right to control that soul; to set our will, as will, in place of its will; to be law unto its life; to try to make of it what it suits our fancy or our convenience to have it; to claim that it is under obligation to us!

The truth is, all the obligation, in the outset, is the other way. We owe all to them. All that we can do to give them happiness, to spare them pain; all that we can do to make them wise and good and safe, — all is too little! All and more than all can never repay them for the sweetness, the blessedness, the development that it has been to us to call children ours. If we can also so win their love by our loving, so deserve their respect by our honorableness, so earn their gratitude by our helpfulness, that they come to be our "lovers and friends," then, ah! then we have had enough of heaven here to make us willing to postpone the more for which we hope beyond!

But all this comes not of authority, not by command; all this is perilled always, always impaired, and often lost, by authoritative, arbitrary ruling, substitution of law and penalty for influence.

It will be objected by parents who disagree with this theory that only authority can prevent license; that without command there will not be control. No one has a right to condemn methods he has not tried. I know, for I have seen, I know, for I have myself tested, that command and authority are short-lived; that they do not insure the results they aim at; that real and permanent control of a child's behavior, even in little things, is gained only by influence, by a slow, sure educating, enlightening, and strengthening of a child's will. I know, for I have seen, that it is possible in this way to make a child only ten years old quite as intelligent and trustworthy a free agent as his mother; to make him so sensible, so gentle, so considerate that to say "must" or "must not" to him would be as unnecessary and absurd as to say it to her.

But, if it be wiser and better to surround even little children with this atmosphere of freedom, how much more essential is it for those who remain under the parental roof long after they have ceased to be children! Just here seems to me to be the fatal rock upon which many households make utter shipwreck of their peace. Fathers and mothers who have ruled by authority (let it be as loving as you please, it will still remain an arbitrary rule) in the beginning, never seem to know when their children are children no longer, but have become men and women. In any average family, the position of an unmarried daughter after she is twenty years old becomes less and less what it should be. In case of sons, the question is rarely a practical one; in those exceptional instances where invalidism or some other disability keeps a man helpless for years under his father's roof, his very helplessness is at once his vindication and his shield, and also prevents his feeling manly revolt against the position of unnatural childhood. But in the case of daughters it is very different. Who does not number in his circle of acquaintance many unmarried women, between the ages of thirty and forty, perhaps even older, who have practically little more freedom in the ordering of their own lives than they had when they were eleven? The mother or the father continues just as much the autocratic centre of the family now as of the nursery, thirty years before. Taking into account the chance — no, the certainty — of great differences between parents and children in matters of temperament and taste, it is easy to see that great suffering must result from this; suffering, too, which involves real loss and hindrance to growth. It is really a monstrous wrong; but it seems to be rarely observed by the world, and never suspected by those who are most responsible for it. It is perhaps a question whether the real tyrannies in this life are those that are accredited as such. There are certainly more than even tyrants know!

Every father and mother has it within easy reach to become the intimate friend of the child. Closest, holiest, sweetest of all friendships is this one, which has the closest, holiest tie of blood to underlie the bond of soul. We see it in rare cases, proving itself divine by rising above even the passion of love between man and woman, and carrying men and women unwedded to their graves for sake of love of mother or father. When we realize what such friendship is, it seems incredible that parents can forego it, or can risk losing any shade of its perfectness, for the sake of any indulgence of the habit of command or of gratifying of selfish preference.

In the ideal household of father and mother and adult children, the one great aim of the parents ought to be to supply, as far as possible to each child, that freedom and independence which they have missed the opportunity of securing in homes of their own. The loss of this one thing alone is a bitterer drop in the loneliness of many an unmarried woman than parents, especially fathers, are apt even to dream, — food and clothes and lodgings are so exalted in unthinking estimates. To be without them would be distressingly inconvenient, no doubt; but one can have luxurious provision of both and remain very wretched. Even the body itself cannot thrive if it has no more than these three pottage messes! Freedom to come, go, speak, work, play, — in short, to be one's self, — is to the body more than meat and gold, and to the soul the whole of life.

Just so far as any parent interferes with this freedom of adult children, even in the little things of a single day or a single hour, just so far it is tyranny, and the children are wronged. But just so far as parents help, strengthen, and bestow this freedom on their children, just so far it is justice and kindness, and their relation is cemented into a supreme and unalterable friendship, whose blessedness and whose comfort no words can measure.

THE READY-TO-HALTS.

MR. READY-TO-HALT must have been the most exasperating pilgrim that Great Heart ever dragged over the road to the Celestial City. Mr. Feeble Mind was bad enough; but genuine weakness and organic incapacity appeal all the while to charity and sympathy. If people really cannot walk, they must be carried. Everybody sees that; and all strong people are, or ought to be, ready to lift babies and cripples. There are plenty of such in every parish. The Feeble Minds are unfortunately predisposed to intermarry; and our schools are overrun with the little Masters and Misses Feeble Mind. But, heavy as they are (and they are apt to be fat), they are precious and pleasant friends and neighbors in comparison with the Ready-to-Halts.

The Ready-to-Halts are never ready for any thing else. They can walk as well as anybody else, if they only would; but they are never quite sure on which road they would better go. Great Hearts have to go back, and go back, to look them up. They are found standing still, helpless and bewildered, on all sorts of absurd side-paths, which lead nowhere; and they never will confess, either, that they need help. They always think they are doing what they call "making up their mind." But, whichever way they make it, they wish they had made it the other; so they unmake it directly. And by this time the crisis of the first hour which they lost has become complicated with that of the second hour, for which they are in no wise ready; and so the hours stumble on, one after another, and the day is only a tangle of ineffective cross purposes. Hundreds of such days drift on, with their sad burden of wasted time. Year after year their lives fail of growth, of delight, of blessing to others. Opportunity's great golden doors, which never stay long open for any man, have always just closed when they reach the threshold of a deed; and it is hard, very hard, to see why it would not have been better for them if they had never been born.

After all, it is not right to be impatient with them; for, in nine cases out of ten, they are no more responsible for their mental limp than the poor Chinese woman is for her feeble feet. From their infancy up to what in our comic caricature of words we call "maturity," they have been bandaged. How should their muscles be good for any thing? From the day when we give, and take, and arrange the baby's playthings for him, hour by hour, without ever setting before him to choose one of two and give up the other, to the day when we take it upon ourselves to decide whether he shall be an engineer or a lawyer, we persist in doing for him the work which he should do for himself. This is because we love him more than we love our own lives. Oh ! if love could but have its eyes opened and see ! If we were not blind, we should know that whenever a child decides for himself deliberately, and without bias from others, any question, however small, he has had just so many minutes of mental gymnastics, — just so much strengthening of the one faculty on whose health and firmness his success in life will depend more than upon any other thing.

So many people do not know the difference between obstinacy and clear-headed firmness of will, that it is hardly safe to say much in praise or blame of either without expressly stating that you do not mean the other. They are as unlike as digestion and indigestion, and one would suppose could not be much more easily confounded ; but it is constantly done. It has not yet ceased to be said among fathers and mothers that it is necessary to " break the will " of children ; and it has not yet ceased to be seen in the land that men by virtue of simple obstinacy are called men of strong character. The truth is that the stronger, better-trained will a man has, the less obstinate he will be. Will is of reason ; obstinacy, of temper. What have they in common ?

For want of strong will kingdoms and souls have been lost. Without it there is no kingdom for any man, — no, not even in his own soul. It is the one attribute of all we possess which is most God-like. By it, we say, under his laws, as he says, enacting those laws, " So far and no further." It is not enough that we do not " break " this grand power. It should be strengthened, developed, trained. And, as the good teacher of gymnastics gives his beginners light weights to lift and swing, so should we bring to the children small points to decide ; to the very little children, very little points. " Will you have the apple, or the orange ? You cannot have both. Choose ; but after you have chosen you cannot change." " Will you have the horseback ride to-day, or the opera to-morrow night ? You can have but one."

Every day, many times a day, a child should decide for himself points involving pros and cons, — substantial ones too. Let him even decide unwisely, and take the consequences ; that too is good for him. No amount of Blackstone can give such an idea of law as a month of prison. Tell him as much as you please of what you know on both sides ; but compel him to decide, and also compel him not to be too long about it. "Choose ye this day whom ye will serve" is a text good for every morning.

If men and women had in their childhood such training of their wills as this, we should not see so many putting their hands to the plough and looking back, and "not fit for the kingdom of heaven." Nor for any kingdom of earth, either, unless it be for the wicked little kingdom of the Prince of Monaco, where there are but two things to be done, — gamble, or drown yourself.

THE DESCENDANTS OF NABAL.

THE line has never been broken, and they have married into respectable families, right and left, until to-day there can hardly be found a household which has not at least one to worry it.

They are not men and women of great passionate natures, who flame out now and then in an outbreak like a volcano, from which everybody runs. This, though terrible while it lasts, is soon over, and there are great compensations in such souls. Their love is worth having. Their tenderness is great. One can forgive them "seventy times seven," for the hasty words and actions of which they repent immediately with tears.

But the Nabals are sullen ; they are grumblers ; they are never done. Such sons of Belial are they to this day that no man can speak peaceably unto them. They are as much worse than passionate people as a slow drizzle of rain is than a thunder-storm. For the thunder-storm, you stay in-doors, and you cannot help having pleasure in its sharp lights and darks and echoes ; and when it is over, what clear air, what a rainbow! But in the drizzle, you go out; you think that with a waterproof, an umbrella, and overshoes, you can manage to get about in spite of it, and attend to your business. What a state you come home in, — muddy, limp, chilled, disheartened! The house greets you, looking also muddy and cold, — for the best of front halls gives up in despair and cannot look any thing but forlorn in a long, drizzling rain; all the windows are bleared with trickling, foggy wet on the outside, which there is no wiping off nor seeing through, and if one could see through there is no gain. The street is more gloomy than the house; black, slimy mud, inches deep on crossings; the same black, slimy mud in footprints on sidewalks; hopeless-looking people hurrying by, so unhappy by reason of the drizzle that a weird sort of family likeness is to be seen in all their faces. This is all that can be seen outside. It is better not to look. For the inside is no redemption except a wood-fire, — a good, generous wood-fire, — not in any of the modern compromises called open stoves, but on a broad stone hearth, with a big background of chimney, up which the sparks can go skipping and creeping.

This can redeem a drizzle; but this cannot redeem a grumbler. Plump he sits down in the warmth of its very blaze, and complains that it snaps, perhaps, or that it is oak and maple, when he paid for all hickory. You can trust him to put out your wood-fire for you as effectually as a water-spout. And, if even a wood-fire, bless it! cannot outshine the gloom of his presence, what is to happen in the places where there is no wood-fire, on the days when real miseries, big and little, are on hand, to be made into mountains of torture by his grumbling?

Oh, who can describe him? There is no language which can do justice to him; no supernatural foresight which can predict where his next thrust will fall, from what unsuspected corner he will send his next arrow. Like death, he has all seasons for his own; his ingenuity is infernal. Whoever tries to forestall or appease him might better be at work in Augean stables; because, after all, we must admit that the facts of life are on his side. It is not intended that we shall be very comfortable. There is a terrible amount of total depravity in animate and inanimate things. From morning till night there is not an hour without its cross to carry. The weather thwarts us; servants, landlords, drivers, washerwomen, and bosom friends misbehave; clothes don't fit; teeth ache; stomachs get out of order; newspapers are stupid; and children make too much noise. If there are not big troubles, there are little ones. If they are not in sight, they are hiding. I have wondered whether the happiest mortal could point to one single moment and say, "At that moment there was nothing in my life which I would have had changed." I think not.

In argument, therefore, the grumbler has the best of it. It is more than probable that things are as he says. But why say it? Why make four miseries out of three? If the three be already unbearable, so much the worse. If he is uncomfortable, it is a pity; we are sorry, but we cannot change the course of Nature. We shall soon have our own little turn of torments, and we do not want to be worn out before it comes by having listened to his; probably, too, the very things of which he complains are pressing just as heavily on us as on him, — are just as unpleasant to everybody as to him. Suppose everybody did as he does. Imagine, for instance, a chorus of grumble from ten people at a breakfast-table, all saying at once, or immediately after each other, "This coffee is not fit to drink." "Really, the attendance in this house is insufferably poor." I have sometimes wished to try this homœopathic treatment in a bad case of grumble. It sounds as if it might work a cure.

If you lose your temper with the grumbler, and turn upon him suddenly, saying, "Oh, do not spoil all our pleasure. Do make the best of things: or, at least, keep quiet!" then how aggrieved he is! how unjust he thinks you are to "make a personal matter of it"! "You do not, surely, suppose I think you are responsible for it, do you?" he says, with a lofty air of astonishment at your unreasonable sensitiveness. Of course, we do not suppose he thinks we are to blame; we do not take him to be a fool as well as a grumbler. But he speaks to us, at us, before us, about the cause of his discomfort, whatever it may be, precisely as he would if we were to blame; and that is one thing which makes his grumbling so insufferable. But this he can never be made to see. And the worst of it is that grumbling is contagious. If we live with him, we shall, sooner or later, in spite of our dislike of his ways, fall into them; even sinking so low, perhaps, before the end of a single summer, as to be heard complaining of butter at boarding-house tables, which is the lowest deep of vulgarity of grumbling. There is no help for this; I have seen it again and again. I have caught it myself. One grumbler in a family is as pestilent a thing as a diseased animal in a herd: if he be not shut up or killed, the herd is lost.

But the grumbler cannot be shut up or killed, since grumbling is not held to be a proof of insanity, nor a capital offence, — more's the pity.

What, then, is to be done? Keep out of his way, at all costs, if he be grown up. If it be a child, labor day and night, as you would with a tendency to paralysis, or distortion of limb, to prevent this blight on its life.

It sounds extreme to say that a child should never be allowed to express a dislike of any thing which cannot be helped; but I think it is true. I do not mean that it should be positively forbidden or punished, but that it should never pass unnoticed; his attention should be invariably called to its uselessness, and to the annoyance it gives to other people. Children begin by being good-natured little grumblers at every thing which goes wrong, simply from the outspokenness of their natures. All they think they say and act. The rudiments of good behavior have to be chiefly negative at the outset, like Punch's advice to those about to marry, — "Don't."

The race of grumblers would soon die out if all children were so trained that never, between the ages of five and twelve, did they utter a needless complaint without being gently reminded that it was foolish and disagreeable. How easy for a good-natured and watchful mother to do this! It takes but a word.

"Oh, dear! I wish it had not rained to-day. It is too bad!"

"You do not really mean what you say, my darling. It is of much more consequence that the grass should grow than that you should go out to play. And it is so silly to complain, when we cannot stop its raining."

"Mamma, I hate this pie."

"Oh! hush, dear! Don't say so, if you do. You can leave it. You need not eat it. But think how disagreeable it sounds to hear you say such a thing."

"Oh, dear! Oh, dear! I am too cold."

"Yes, dear, I know you are. So is mamma. But we shall not feel any warmer for saying so. We must wait till the fire burns better; and the time will seem twice as long if we grumble."

"Oh, mamma! mamma! My steam-engine is all spoiled. It won't run. I hate things that wind up!"

"But, my dear little boy, don't grumble so! What would you think if mamma were to say, 'Oh, dear! oh, dear! My little boy's stockings are full of holes. How I hate to mend stockings!' and, 'Oh, dear! oh, dear! My little boy has upset my work-box! I hate little boys'?"

How they look steadily into your eyes for a minute, — the honest, reasonable little souls! — when you say such things to them; and then run off with a laugh, lifted up, for that time, by your fitly spoken words of help.

Oh! if the world could only stop long enough for one generation of mothers to be made all right, what a millennium could be begun in thirty years!

"But, mamma, you are grumbling yourself at me because I grumbled!" says a quick-witted darling not ten years old. Ah! never shall any weak spot in our armor escape the keen eyes of these little ones.

"Yes, dear! And I shall grumble at you till I cure you of grumbling. Grumblers are the only thing in this world that it is right to grumble at."

"BOYS NOT ALLOWED."

IT was a conspicuous signboard, at least four feet long, with large black letters on a white ground: "Boys not allowed." I looked at it for some moments in a sort of bewildered surprise: I did not quite comprehend the meaning of the words. At last I understood it. I was waiting in a large railway station, where many trains connect; and most of the passengers from the train in which I was were eating dinner in a hotel near by. I was entirely alone in the car, with the exception of one boy, who was perhaps eleven years old. I made an involuntary ejaculation as I read the words on the sign, and the boy looked around at me.

"Little boy," said I, solemnly, "do you see that sign?"

He turned his head, and, reading the ominous warning, nodded sullenly, but said nothing.

"Boy, what does it mean?" said I. "Boys must be allowed to come into this railway station. There are two now standing in the doorway directly under the sign."

The latent sympathy in my tone touched his heart.

He left his seat, and, coming to mine, edged in past me ; and, putting his head out of the window, read the sentence aloud in a contemptuous tone. Then he offered me a peanut, which I took ; and he proceeded to tell me what he thought of the sign.

"Boys not allowed!" said he. "That's just the way 'tis everywhere ; but I never saw the sign up before. It don't make any difference, though, whether they put the sign up or not. Why, in New York (you live in New York, don't you?) they won't even stop the horse-cars for a boy to get on. Nobody thinks any thing'll hurt a boy ; but they're glad enough to 'allow' us when there's any errands to be done, and" —

"Do you live in New York?" interrupted I ; for I did not wish to hear the poor little fellow's list of miseries, which I knew by heart beforehand without his telling me, having been hopeless knight-errant of oppressed boyhood all my life.

Yes, he "lived in New York," and he "went to a grammar school," and he had "two sisters." And so we talked on in that sweet, ready, trustful talk which comes naturally only from children's lips, until the "twenty minutes for refreshments" were over, and the choked and crammed passengers, who had eaten big dinners in that breath of time, came hurrying back to their seats. Among them came the father and mother of my little friend. In angry surprise at not finding him in the seat where they left him, they exclaimed, —

"Now, where *is* that boy? Just like him! We might have lost every one of these bags."

"Here I am, mamma," he called out, pleasantly. "I could see the bags all the time. Nobody came into the car."

"I told you not to leave the seat, sir. What do you mean by such conduct?" said the father.

"Oh, no, papa," said poor Boy, "you only told me to take care of the bags." And an anxious look of terror came into his face, which told only too well under how severe a *régime* he lived. I interposed hastily with—

"I am afraid I am the cause of your little son's leaving his seat. He had sat very still till I spoke to him; and I believe I ought to take all the blame."

The parents were evidently uncultured, shallow people. Their irritation with him was merely a surface vexation, which had no real foundation in a deep principle. They became complaisant and smiling at my first word, and Boy escaped with a look of great relief to another seat, where they gave him a simple luncheon of saleratus gingerbread. "Boys not allowed" to go in to dinner at the Massasoit, thought I to myself; and upon that text I sat sadly meditating all the way from Springfield to Boston.

How true it was, as the little fellow had said, that "it don't make any difference whether they put the sign up or not!" No one can watch carefully any average household where there are boys, and not see that there are a thousand little ways in which the boys' comfort, freedom, preference will be disregarded, when the girls' will be considered. This is partly intentional, partly unconscious. Something is to be said undoubtedly on the advantage of making the boy realize early and keenly that manhood is to bear and to work, and womanhood is to be helped and sheltered. But this should be inculcated, not inflicted; asked, not seized; shown and explained, not commanded. Nothing can be surer than the growth in a boy of tender, chivalrous regard for his sisters and for all women, if the seeds of it be rightly sown and gently nurtured. But the common method is quite other than this. It begins too harshly and at once with assertion or assumption.

"Mother never thinks I am of any consequence," said a dear boy to me, the other day. "She's all for the girls."

This was not true; but there was truth in it. And I am very sure that the selfishness, the lack of real courtesy, which we see so plainly and pitiably in the behavior of the average young man to-day is the slow, certain result of years of just such feelings as this child expressed. The boy has to scramble for his rights. Naturally he is too busy to think much about the rights of others. The man keeps up the habit, and is negatively selfish without knowing it.

Take, for instance, the one point of the minor courtesies (if we can dare to call any courtesies minor) of daily intercourse. How many people are there who habitually speak to a boy of ten, twelve, or fourteen with the same civility as to his sister, a little younger or older?

"I like Miss ——," said this same dear boy to me, one day; "for she always bids me good-morning."

Ah! never is one such word thrown away on a loving, open-hearted boy. Men know that safe through all the wear and tear of life they keep far greener the memory of some woman or some man who was kind to them in their boyhood than of the friend who helped or cheered them yesterday.

Dear, blessed, noisy, rollicking, tormenting, comforting Boy! What should we do without him? How much we like, without suspecting it, his breezy presence in the house! Except for him, how would errands be done, chairs brought, nails driven, cows stoned out of our way, letters carried, twine and knives kept ready, lost things found, luncheon carried to picnics, three-year-olds that cry led out of meeting, butterflies and birds' nests and birch-bark got, the horse taken round to the stable, borrowed things sent home, — and all with no charge for time?

Dear, patient, busy Boy! Shall we not sometimes answer his questions? Give him a comfortable seat? Wait and not reprove him till after the company has gone? Let him wear his best jacket, and buy him half as many neckties as his sister has? Give him some honey, even if there is not enough to go round? Listen tolerantly to his little bragging, and help him "do" his sums?

With a sudden shrill scream the engine slipped off on a side-track, and the cars glided into the great, grim city-station, looking all the grimmer for its twinkling lights. The masses of people who were waiting and the masses of people who had come surged toward each other like two great waves, and mingled in a moment. I caught sight of my poor little friend, Boy, following his father, struggling along in the crowd, carrying two heavy carpet-bags, a strapped bundle, and two umbrellas, and being sharply told to "Keep up close there."

"Ha!" said I, savagely, to myself, "doing porters' work is not one of the things which 'boys' are 'not allowed.'"

HALF AN HOUR IN A RAILWAY STATION.

IT was one of those bleak and rainy days which mark the coming of spring on New England sea-shores. The rain felt and looked as if it might at any minute become hail or snow; the air pricked like needles when it blew against flesh. Yet the huge railway station was as full of people as ever. One could see no difference between this dreariest of days and the sunniest, so far as the crowd was concerned, except that fewer of the people wore fine clothes; perhaps, also, that their faces looked a little more sombre and weary than usual.

There is no place in the world where human nature shows to such sad disadvantage as in waiting-rooms at railway stations, especially in the "Ladies' Room." In the "Gentlemen's Room" there is less of that ghastly, apathetic silence which seems only explainable as an interval between two terrible catastrophes. Shall we go so far as to confess that even the unsightly spittoons, and the uncleanly and loquacious fellowship resulting from their common use, seem here, for the moment, redeemed from a little of their abominableness, — simply because almost any action is better than utter inaction, and any thing which makes the joyless, taciturn American speak to his fellow whom he does not know, is for the time being a blessing. But in the " Ladies' Room " there is not even a community of interest in a single bad habit, to break the monotone of weary stillness. Who has not felt the very soul writhe within her as she has first crossed the threshold of one of these dismal antechambers of journey? Carpetless, dingy, dusty; two or three low sarcophagi of greenish-gray iron in open spaces, surrounded by blue-lipped women, in different angles and attitudes of awkwardness, trying to keep the soles of their feet in a perpendicular position, to be warmed at what they have been led to believe is a steam-heating apparatus; a few more women, equally listless and weary-looking, standing in equally difficult and awkward positions before a counter, holding pie in one hand, and tea in a cup and saucer in the other, taking alternate mouthfuls of each, and spilling both; the rest wedged bolt upright against the wall in narrow partitioned seats, which only need a length of perforated foot-board in front to make them fit to be patented as the best method of putting whole communities of citizens into the stocks at once. All, feet warmers, pie-eaters, and those who sit in the red-velvet stocks, wear so exactly the same expression of vacuity and fatigue that they might almost be taken for one gigantic and unhappy family connection, on its way to what is called in newspapers "a sad event." The only wonder is that this stiffened, desiccated crowd retains vitality enough to remember the hours at which its several trains depart, and to rise up and shake itself alive and go on board. One is haunted sometimes by the fancy that some day, when the air in the room is unusually bad and the trains are delayed, a curious phenomenon will be seen. The petrifaction will be carried a little farther than usual, and, when the bell rings and the official calls out, "Train made up for Babel, Hinnom, and way stations?" no women will come forth from the "Ladies' Room," no eye will move, no muscle will stir. Husbands and brothers will wait and search vainly for those who should have met them at the station, with bundles of the day's shopping to be carried out; homes will be desolate; and the history of rare fossils and petrifactions will have a novel addition. Or, again, that, if some sudden convulsion of Nature, like those which before now have buried wicked cities and the dwellers in them, were to-day to swallow up the great city of New Sodom in America, and keep it under ground for a few thousand years, nothing in all its circuit would so puzzle the learned archæologists of A. D. 5873 as the position of the skeletons in these same waiting-rooms of railway stations.

Thinking such thoughts as these, sinking slowly and surely to the level of the place, I waited, on this bleak, rainy day, in just such a "Ladies' Room" as I have described. I sat in the red-velvet stocks, with my eyes fixed on the floor.

"Please, ma'am, won't you buy a basket?" said a cheery little voice. So near me, without my knowing it, had the little tradesman come that I was as startled as if the voice had spoken out of the air just above my head.

He was a sturdy little fellow, ten years old, Irish, dirty, ragged; but he had honest, kind gray eyes, and a smile which ought to have sold more baskets than he could carry. A few kind words unsealed the fountain of his childish confidences. There were four children younger than he; the mother took in washing, and the father, who was a cripple from rheumatism, made these baskets, which he carried about to sell.

"Where do you sell the most?"

"Round the depots. That's the best place."

"But the baskets are rather clumsy to carry. Almost everybody has his hands full, when he sets out on a journey."

"Yis'm; but mostly they doesn't take the baskets. But they gives me a little change," said he, with a smile, half roguish, half sad.

I watched him on in his pathetic pilgrimage round that dreary room, seeking help from that dreary circle of women.

My heart aches to write down here the true record that out of those scores of women only three even smiled or spoke to the little fellow. Only one gave him money. My own sympathies had been so won by his face and manner that I found myself growing hot with resentment as I watched woman after woman wave him off with indifferent or impatient gesture. His face was a face which no mother ought to have been able to see without a thrill of pity and affection. God forgive me ! As if any mother ought to be able to see any child, ragged, dirty, poor, seeking help and finding none ! But his face was so honest, and brave, and responsive that it added much to the appeal of his poverty.

One woman, young and pretty, came into the room, bringing in her arms a large toy horse, and a little violin. "Oh," I said to myself, "she has a boy of her own, for whom she can buy gifts freely. She will surely give this poor child a penny." He thought so, too ; for he went toward her with a more confident manner than he had shown to some of the others. No ! She brushed by him impatiently, without a word, and walked to the ticket-office. He stood looking at the violin and the toy horse till she came back to her seat. Then he lifted his eyes to her face again ; but she apparently did not see him, and he went away. Ah, she is only half mother who does not see her own child in every child ! — her own child's grief in every pain which makes another child weep !

Presently the little basket-boy went out into the great hall. I watched him threading his way in and out among the groups of men. I saw one man — bless him ! — pat the little fellow on the head ; then I lost sight of him.

After ten minutes he came back into the Ladies' Room, with only one basket in his hand, and a very happy little face. The "sterner sex" had been kinder to him than we. The smile which he gave me in answer to my glad recognition of his good luck was the sunniest sunbeam I have seen on a human face for many a day. He sank down into the red-velvet stocks, and twirled his remaining basket, and swung his shabby little feet, as idle and unconcerned as if he were some rich man's son, waiting for the train to take him home. So much does a little lift help the heart of a child, even of a beggar child. It is a comfort to remember him, with that look on his face, instead of the wistful, pleading one which I saw at first. I left him lying back on the dusty velvet, which no doubt seemed to him unquestionable splendor. In the cars I sat just behind the woman with the toy-horse and the violin. I saw her glance rest lovingly on them many times, as she thought of her boy at home; and I wondered if the little basket-seller had really produced no impression whatever on her heart. I shall remember him long after (if he lives) he is a man!

A GENIUS FOR AFFECTION.

THE other day, speaking superficially and uncharitably, I said of a woman, whom I knew but slightly, "She disappoints me utterly. How could her husband have married her? She is commonplace and stupid."

"Yes," said my friend, reflectively; "it **is** strange. She is not a brilliant woman; she is not even an intellectual one; but there is such a thing as a genius for affection, and she has it. It has been good for her husband that he married her."

The words sank into my heart like a great spiritual plummet. They dropped down to depths not often stirred. And from those depths came up some shining sands of truth, worth keeping among treasures; having a phosphorescent light in them, which can shine in dark places, and, making them light as day, reveal their beauty.

"A genius for affection." Yes; there is such a thing, and no other genius is so great. The phrase means something more than a capacity, or even a talent for loving. That is common to all human beings, more or less. A man or woman without it would be a monster, such as has probably never been on the earth. All men and women, whatever be their shortcomings in other directions, have this impulse, this faculty, in a degree. It takes shape in family ties: makes clumsy and unfortunate work of them in perhaps two cases out of three, — wives tormenting husbands, husbands neglecting and humiliating wives, parents maltreating and ruining children, children disobeying and grieving parents, and brothers and sisters quarrelling to the point of proverbial mention; but under all this, in spite of all this, the love is there. A great trouble or a sudden emergency will bring it out. In any common danger, hands clasp closely and quarrels are forgotten; over a sick-bed hard ways soften into yearning tenderness; and by a grave, alas! what hot tears fall! The poor, imperfect love which had let itself be wearied and harassed by the frictions of life, or hindered and warped by a body full of diseased nerves, comes running, too late, with its effort to make up lost opportunities. It has been all the while alive, but in a sort of trance; little good has come of it, but it is something that it was there. It is the divine germ of a flower and fruit too precious to mature in the first years after grafting; in other soils, by other waters, when the healing of the nations is fulfilled, we shall see its perfection. Oh! what atonement will be there! What allowances we shall make for each other, then! with what love we shall love!

But the souls who have what my friend meant by a "genius for affection" are in another atmosphere than that which common men breathe. Their "upper air" is clearer, more rarefied than any to which mere intellectual genius can soar. Because, to this last, always remain higher heights which it cannot grasp, see, nor comprehend.

Michel Angelo may build his dome of marble, and human intellect may see as clearly as if God had said it that no other dome can ever be built so grand, so beautiful. But above St. Peter's hangs the blue tent-dome of the sky, vaster, rounder, elastic, unfathomable, making St. Peter's look small as a drinking-cup, shutting it soon out of sight to north, east, south, and west, by the mysterious horizon-fold which no man can lift. And beyond this horizon-fold of our sky shut down again other domes, which the wisest astronomer may not measure, in whose distances our little ball and we, with all our spinning, can hardly show like a star. If St. Peter's were swallowed up to-morrow, it would make no real odds to anybody but the Pope. The probabilities are that Michel Angelo himself has forgotten all about it.

Titian and Raphael, and all the great brotherhood of painters, may kneel reverently as priests before Nature's face, and paint pictures at sight of which all men's eyes shall fill with grateful tears; and yet all men shall go away, and find that the green shade of a tree, the light on a young girl's face, the sleep of a child, the flowering of a flower, are to their pictures as living life to beautiful death.

Coming to Art's two highest spheres, — music of sound and music of speech, — we find that Beethoven and Mozart, and Milton and Shakespeare, have written. But the symphony is sacred only because, and only so far as, it renders the joy or the sorrow which we have felt. Surely, the interpretation is less than the thing interpreted. Face to face with a joy, a sorrow, would a symphony avail us? And, as for words, who shall express their feebleness in midst of strength? The fettered helplessness in spite of which they soar to such heights? The most perfect sentence ever written bears to the thing it meant to say the relation which the chemist's formula does to the thing he handles, names, analyzes, can destroy, perhaps, but cannot make. Every element in the crystal, the liquid, can be weighed, assigned, and rightly called; nothing in all science is more wonderful than an exact chemical formula; but, after all is done, will remain for ever unknown the one subtle secret, the vital centre of the whole.

But the souls who have a "genius for affection" have no outer dome, no higher and more vital beauty; no subtle secret of creative motive force to elude their grasp, mock their endeavor, overshadow their lives. The subtlest essence of the thing they worship and desire, they have in their own nature, — they are. No schools, no standards, no laws can help or hinder them.

To them the world is as if it were not. Work and pain and loss are as if they were not. These are they to whom it is easy to die any death, if good can come that way to one they love. These are they who do die daily unnoted on our right hand and on our left, —

fathers and mothers for children, husbands and wives for each other. These are they, also, who live, — which is often far harder than it is to die, — long lives, into whose being never enters one thought of self from the rising to the going down of the sun. Year builds on year with unvarying steadfastness the divine temple of their beauty and their sacrifice. They create, like God. The universe which science sees, studies, and explains, is small, is petty, beside the one which grows under their spiritual touch; for love begets love. The waves of eternity itself ripple out in immortal circles under the ceaseless dropping of their crystal deeds.

Angels desire to look, but cannot, into the mystery of holiness and beauty which such human lives reveal. Only God can see them clearly. God is their nearest of kin; for He is love.

RAINY DAYS.

WITH what subtle and assured tyranny they take possession of the world! Stoutest hearts are made subject, plans of conquerors set aside, — thc heavens and the earth and man, — all alike at the mercy of the rain. Come when they may, wait long as they will, give what warnings they can, rainy days are always interruptions. No human being has planned for them then and there. "If it had been but yesterday," "If it were only to-morrow," is the cry from all lips. Ah! a lucky tyranny for us is theirs. Were the clouds subject to mortal call or prohibition, the seasons would fail and death get upper hand of all things before men agreed on an hour of common convenience.

What tests they are of people's souls! Show me a dozen men and women in the early morning of a rainy day, and I will tell by their words and their faces who among them is rich and who is poor,—who has much goods laid up for just such times of want, and who has been spendthrift and foolish. That curious, shrewd, underlying instinct, common to all ages, which takes shape in proverbs recognized this long ago. Who knows when it was first said of a man laying up money, "He lays by for a rainy day"? How close the parallel is between the man who, having spent on each day's living the whole of each day's income, finds himself helpless in an emergency of sickness whose expenses he has no money to meet, and the man who, having no intellectual resources, no self-reliant habit of occupation, finds himself shut up in the house idle and wretched for a rainy day. I confess that on rainy mornings in country houses, among well-dressed and so-called intelligent and Christian people, I have been seized with stronger disgusts and despairs about the capacity and worth of the average human creature, than I have ever felt in the worst haunts of ignorant wickedness.

"What is there to do to-day?" is the question they ask. I know they are about to ask it before they speak. I have seen it in their listless and disconcerted eyes at breakfast. It is worse to me than the tolling of a bell; for saddest dead of all are they who have only a "name to live."

The truth is, there is more to do on a rainy day than on any other. In addition to all the sweet, needful, possible business of living and working, and learning and helping, which is for all days, there is the beauty of the rainy day to see, the music of the rainy day to hear. It drums on the window-panes, chuckles and gurgles at corners of houses, tinkles in spouts, makes mysterious crescendoes and arpeggio chords through the air; and all the while drops from the eaves and upper window-ledges are beating time as rhythmical and measured as that of a metronome, — time to which our own souls furnish tune, sweet or sorrowful, inspiriting or saddening, as we will. It is a curious experiment to try repeating or chanting lines in time and cadence following the patter of raindrops on windows. It will sometimes be startling in its effect: no metre, no accent fails of its response in the low, liquid stroke of the tender drops,—there seems an uncanny *rapport* between them at once.

And the beauty of the rain, not even love can find words to tell it. If it left but one trace, the exquisite shifting sheen of pearls on the outer side of the window glass, that alone one might watch for a day. In all times it has been thought worthy of kings, of them who are royally rich, to have garments sown thick in dainty lines and shapes with fine seed pearls. Who ever saw any such embroidery which could compare with the beauty of one pane of glass wrought on a single side with the shining white transparent globulets of rain? They are millions; they crowd; they blend; they become a silver stream; they glide slowly down, leaving tiniest silver threads behind; they make of themselves a silver bank of miniature sea at the bottom of the pane; and, while they do this, other millions are set pearl-wise at the top, to crowd, blend, glide down in their turn, and overflow the miniature sea. This is one pane, a few inches square; and rooms have many windows of many panes. And looking past this spectacle, out of our windows, how is it that we do not each rainy day weep with pleasure at sight of the glistening show? Every green thing, from tiniest grass-blade lying lowest, to highest waving tips of elms, also set thick with the water-pearls ; all tossing and catching, and tossing and catching, in fairy game with the wind, and with the rain itself, always losing, always gaining, changing shape and place and number every moment, till the twinkling and shifting dazzle all eyes.

Then at the end comes the sun, like a magician for whom all had been made ready ; at sunset, perhaps, or at sunrise, if the storm has lasted all night. In one instant the silver balls begin to disappear. By countless thousands at a time he tosses them back whence they came ; but as they go, he changes them, under our eyes, into prismatic globes, holding very light of very light in their tiny circles, shredding and sorting it into blazing lines of rainbow color.

All the little children shout with delight, seeing these things ; and call dull, grown-up people to behold. They reply, "Yes, the storm is over ; " and this is all it means to most of them. This kingdom of heaven they cannot enter, not being "as a little child."

It would be worth while to know, if we only could, just what our betters — the birds and insects and beasts — do on rainy days. But we cannot find out much. It would be a great thing to look inside of an ant-hill in a long rain. All we know is that the doors are shut tight, and a few sentinels, who look as if India-rubber coats would be welcome, stand outside. The stillness and look of intermission in the woods on a really rainy day is something worth getting wet to observe. It is like Sunday in London, or Fourth of

July in a country town which has gone bodily to a picnic in the next village. The strays who are out seem like accidentally arrived people, who have lost their way. One cannot fancy a caterpillar's being otherwise than very uncomfortable in wet hair; and what can there be for butterflies and dragon-flies to do, in the close corners into which they creep, with wings shut up as tight as an umbrella? The beasts fare better, being clothed in hides. Those whom we oftenest see out in rains (cows and oxen and horses) keep straight on with their perpetual munching, as content wet as dry, though occasionally we see them accept the partial shelter of a tree from a particularly hard shower.

Hens are the forlornest of all created animals when it rains. Who can help laughing at sight of a flock of them huddled up under lee of a barn, limp, draggled, spiritless, shifting from one leg to the other, with their silly heads hanging inert to right or left, looking as if they would die for want of a yawn? One sees just such groups of other two-legged creatures in parlors, under similar circumstances. The truth is, a hen's life at best seems poorer than that of any other known animal. Except when she is setting, I cannot help having a contempt for her. This also has been recognized by that common instinct of people which goes to the making of proverbs; for "Hen's time ain't worth much" is a common saying among farmers' wives. How she dawdles about all day, with her eyes not an inch from the ground, forever scratching and feeding in dirtiest places, — a sort of animated muck-rake, with a mouth and an alimentary canal! No wonder such an inane creature is wretched when it rains, and her soulless business is interrupted. She is, I think, likest of all to the human beings, men or women, who do not know what to do with themselves on rainy days.

FRIENDS OF THE PRISONERS.

IN many of the Paris prisons is to be seen a long, dreary room, through the middle of which are built two high walls of iron grating, enclosing a spâce of some three feet in width.

A stranger visiting the prison for the first time would find it hard to divine for what purpose these walls of grating had been built. But on the appointed days when the friends of the prisoners are allowed to enter the prison, their use is sadly evident. It would nòt be safe to permit wives and husbands, and mothers and sons, to clasp hands in unrestrained freedom. A tiny file, a skein of silk, can open prison-doors and set captives free; love's ingenuity will circumvent tyranny and fetters, in spite of all possible precautions. Therefore the vigilant authority says, "You may see, but not touch; there shall be no possible opportunity for an instrument of escape to be given; at more than arm's length the wife, the mother must be held." The prisoners are led in and seated on a bench upon one side of these gratings; the friends are led in and seated on a similar bench on the other side; jailers are in attendance in both rooms; no words can be spoken which the jailers do not hear. Yearningly eyes meet eyes; faces are pressed against the hard wires; loving words are exchanged; the poor prisoned souls ask eagerly for news from the outer world, — the world from which they are as much hidden as if they were dead. Fathers hear how the little ones have grown; sometimes, alas! how the little ones have died. Small gifts of fruit or clothing are brought; but must be given first into the hands of the jailers. Even flowers cannot be given from loving hand to hand; for in the tiniest flower might be hidden the secret poison which would give to the weary prisoner surest escape of all. All day comes and goes the sad train of friends; lingering and turning back after there is no more to be said; weeping when they meant and tried to smile; more hungry for closer sight and voice, and for touch, with every moment that they gaze through the bars; and going away, at last, with a new sense of loss and separation, which time, with its merciful healing, will hardly soften before the visiting-day will come again, and the same heart-rending experience of mingled torture and joy will again be borne. But to the prisoners these glimpses of friends' faces are like manna from heaven. Their whole life, physical and mental, receives a new impetus from them. Their blood flows more quickly, their eyes light up, they live from one day to the next on a memory and a hope. No punishment can be invented so terrible as the deprivation of the sight of their friends on the visiting-day. Men who are obstinate and immovable before any sort or amount of physical torture are subdued by mere threat of this.

A friend who told me of a visit he paid to the Prison Mazas, on one of the days, said, with tears in his eyes, "It was almost more than I could bear to see these poor souls reaching out toward each other from either side of the iron railings. Here a poor, old woman, tottering and weak, bringing a little fruit in a basket for her son; here a wife, holding up a baby to look through the gratings at its father, and the father trying in an agony of earnestness to be sure that the baby knew him; here a little girl, looking half reproachfully at her brother, terror struggling with tenderness in her young face; on the side of the friends, love and yearning and pity beyond all words to describe; on the side of the prisoners, love and yearning just as great, but with a misery of shame added, which gave to many faces a look of attempt at dogged indifference on the surface, constantly betrayed and contradicted, however, by the flashing of the eyes and the red of the cheeks."

The story so impressed me that I could not for days lose sight of the picture it raised; the double walls of iron grating; the cruel, inexorable, empty space between them, — empty, yet crowded with words and looks; the lines of anxious, yearning faces on either side. But presently I said to myself, It is, after all, not so unlike the life we all live. Who of us is not in prison? Who of us is not living out his time of punishment? Law holds us all in its merciless fulfilment of penalty for sin; disease, danger, work separate us, wall us, bury us. That we are not numbered with the number of a cell, clothed in the uniform of a prison, locked up at night, and counted in the morning, is only an apparent difference, and not so real a one. Our jailers do not know us; but we know them. There is no fixed day gleaming for us in the future when our term of sentence will expire and we shall regain freedom. It may be to-morrow; but it may be three-score years away. Meantime, we bear ourselves as if we were not in prison. We profess that we choose, we keep our fetters out of sight, we smile, we sing, we contrive to be glad of being alive, and we take great interest in the changing of our jails. But no man knows where his neighbor's prison lies. How bravely and cheerily most eyes look up! This is one of the sweetest mercies of life, that "the heart knoweth its own bitterness," and, knowing it, can hide it. Hence, we can all be friends for other prisoners, standing separated from them by the impassable iron gratings and the fixed gulf of space, which are not inappropriate emblems of the unseen barriers between all human souls. We can show kindly faces, speak kindly words, bear to them fruits and food, and moral help, greater than fruit or food. We need not aim at philanthropies; we need not have a visiting-day, nor seek a prison-house built of stone. On every road each man we meet is a prisoner; he is dying at heart, however sound he looks; he is only waiting, however well he works. If we stop to ask whether he be our brother, he is gone. Our one smile would have lit up his prison-day. Alas for us if we smiled not as we passed by! Alas for us if, face to face, at last, with our Elder Brother, we find ourselves saying, "Lord, when saw we thee sick and in prison!"

A COMPANION FOR THE WINTER.

I HAVE engaged a companion for the winter. It would be simply a superfluous egotism to say this to the public, except that I have a philanthropic motive for doing so. There are many lonely people who are in need of a companion possessing just such qualities as his; and he has brothers singularly like himself, whose services can be secured. I despair of doing justice to him by any description. In fact, thus far, I discover new perfections in him daily, and believe that I am yet only on the threshold of our friendship.

In conversation he is more suggestive than any person I have ever known. After two or three hours alone with him, I am sometimes almost startled to look back and see through what a marvellous train of fancy and reflection he has led me. Yet he is never wordy, and often conveys his subtlest meaning by a look.

He is an artist, too, of the rarest sort. You watch the process under which his pictures grow with incredulous wonder. The Eastern magic which drops the seed in the mould, and bids it shoot up before your eyes, blossom, and bear its fruit in an hour, is tardy and clumsy by side of the creative genius of my companion. His touch is swift as air; his coloring is vivid as light; he has learned, I know not how, the secrets of hidden places in all lands; and he paints, now a tufted clump of soft cocoa palms; now the spires and walls of an iceberg, glittering in yellow sunlight; now a desolate, sandy waste, where black rocks and a few crumbling ruins are lit up by a lurid glow; then a cathedral front, with carvings like lace; then the skeleton of a wrecked ship, with bare ribs and broken masts, — and all so exact, so minute, so life-like, that you believe no man could paint thus any thing which he had not seen.

He has a special love for mosaics, and a marvellous faculty for making drawings of curious old patterns. Nothing is too complicated for his memory, and he revels in the most fantastic and intricate shapes. I have known him in a single evening throw off a score of designs, all beautiful, and many of them rare: fiery scorpions on a black ground; pale lavender filagrees over scarlet; white and black squares blocked out as for tiles of a pavement, and crimson and yellow threads interlaced over them; odd Chinese patterns in brilliant colors, all angles and surprises, with no likeness to any thing in nature; and exquisite little bits of landscape in soft grays and whites. Last night was one of his nights of reminiscences of the mosaic-workers. A furious snow-storm was raging, and, as the flaky crystals piled up in drifts on the window-ledges, he seemed to catch the inspiration of their law of structure, and drew sheet after sheet of crystalline shapes; some so delicate and filmy that it seemed as if a jar might obliterate them; some massive and strong, like those in which the earth keeps her mineral treasures; then, at last, on a round charcoal disk, he traced out a perfect rose, in a fragrant white powder, which piled up under his fingers, petal after petal, circle after circle, till the feathery stamens were buried out of sight. Then, as we held our breath for fear of disturbing it, with a good-natured little chuckle, he shook it off into the fire, and by a few quick strokes of red turned the black charcoal disk into a shield gay enough for a tournament.

He has talent for modelling, but this he exercises more rarely. Usually, his figures are grotesque rather than beautiful, and he never allows them to remain longer than for a few moments, often changing them so rapidly under your eye that it seems like jugglery. He is fondest of doing this at twilight, and loves the darkest corner of the room. From the half-light he will suddenly thrust out before you a grinning gargoyle head, to which he will give in an instant more a pair of spider legs, and then, with one roll, stretch it out into a crocodile, whose jaws seem so near snapping that you involuntarily draw your chair further back. Next, in a freak of ventriloquism, he startles you still more by bringing from the crocodile's mouth a sigh, so long drawn, so human, that you really shudder, and are ready to implore him to play no more tricks. He knows when he has reached this limit, and soothes you at once by a tender, far-off whisper, like the wind through pines, sometimes almost like an Æolian harp; then he rouses you from your dreams by what you are sure is a tap at the door. You turn, speak, listen; no one enters; the tap again. Ah! it is only a little more of the ventriloquism of this wonderful creature. You are alone with him, and there was no tap at the door.

But when there is, and the friend comes in, then my companion's genius shines out. Almost always in life the third person is a discord, or at least a burden; but he is so genial, so diffusive, so sympathetic, that, like some tints by which painters know how to bring out all the other colors in a picture, he forces every one to do his best. I am indebted to him already for a better knowledge of some men and women with whom I had talked for years before to little purpose. It is most wonderful that he produces this effect, because he himself is so silent; but there is some secret charm in his very smile which puts people *en rapport* with each other, and with him at once.

I am almost afraid to go on with the list of the things my companion can do. I have not yet told the half, nor the most wonderful; and I believe I have already overtaxed credulity. I will mention only one more, — but that is to me far more inexplicable than all the rest. I am sure that it belongs, with mesmerism and clairvoyance, to the domain of the higher psychological mysteries. He has in rare hours the power of producing the portraits of persons whom you have loved, but whom he has never seen. For this it is necessary that you should concentrate your whole attention on him, as is always needful to secure the best results of mesmeric power. It must also be late and still. In the day, or in a storm, I have never known him to succeed in this. For these portraits he uses only shadowy gray tints. He begins with a hesitating outline. If you are not tenderly and closely in attention, he throws it aside; he can do nothing. But if you are with him, heart and soul, and do not take your eyes from his, he will presently fill out the dear faces, full, life-like, and wearing a smile, which makes you sure that they too must have been summoned from the other side, as you from this, to meet on the shadowy boundary between flesh and spirit. He must see them as clearly as he sees you; and it would be little more for his magic to do if he were at the same moment showing to their longing eyes your face and answering smile.

But I delay too long the telling of his name. A strange hesitancy seizes me. I shall never be believed by any one who has not sat as I have by his side. But, if I can only give to one soul the good-cheer and strength of such a presence, I shall be rewarded.

His name is Maple Wood-fire, and his terms are from eight to twelve dollars a month, according to the amount of time he gives. This price is ridiculously low, but it is all that any member of the family asks; in fact, in some parts of the country, they can be hired for much less. They have connections by the name of Hickory, whose terms are higher; but I cannot find out that they are any more satisfactory. There are also some distant relations, named Chestnut and Pine, who can be employed in the same way, at a much lower rate; but they are all snappish and uncertain in temper.

To the whole world I commend the good brotherhood of Maple, and pass on the emphatic indorsement of a blessed old black woman who came to my room the other day, and, standing before the rollicking blaze on my hearth, said, "Bless yer, honey, yer's got a wood-fire. I'se allers said that, if yer's got a wood-fire, yer's got meat, an' drink, an' clo'es."

CHOICE OF COLORS.

THE other day, as I was walking on one of the oldest and most picturesque streets of the old and picturesque town of Newport, R. I., I saw a little girl standing before the window of a milliner's shop.

It was a very rainy day. The pavement of the sidewalks on this street is so sunken and irregular that in wet weather, unless one walks with very great care, he steps continually into small wells of water. Up to her ankles in one of these wells stood the little girl, apparently as unconscious as if she were high and dry before a fire. It was a very cold day too. I was hurrying along, wrapped in furs, and not quite warm enough even so. The child was but thinly clothed. She wore an old plaid shawl and a ragged knit hood of scarlet worsted. One little red ear stood out unprotected by the hood, and drops of water trickled down over it from her hair. She seemed to be pointing with her finger at articles in the window, and talking to some one inside. I watched her for several moments, and then crossed the street to see what it all meant. I stole noiselessly up behind her, and she did not hear me. The window was full of artificial flowers, of the cheapest sort, but of very gay colors. Here and there a knot of ribbon or a bit of lace had been tastefully added, and the whole effect was really remarkably gay and pretty. Tap, tap, tap, went the small hand against the window-pane; and with every tap the unconscious little creature murmured, in a half-whispering, half-singing voice, "I choose *that* color." "I choose *that* color." "I choose *that* color."

I stood motionless. I could not see her face; but there was in her whole attitude and tone the heartiest content and delight. I moved a little to the right, hoping to see her face, without her seeing me; but the slight movement caught her ear, and in a second she had sprung aside and turned toward me. The spell was broken. She was no longer the queen of an air-castle, decking herself in all the rainbow hues which pleased her eye. She was a poor beggar child, out in the rain, and a little frightened at the approach of a stranger. She did not move away, however; but stood eying me irresolutely, with that pathetic mixture of interrogation and defiance in her face which is so often seen in the prematurely developed faces of poverty-stricken children.

"Aren't the colors pretty?" I said. She brightened instantly.

"Yes'm. I'd like a goon av thit blue."

"But you will take cold standing in the wet," said I. "Won't you come under my umbrella?"

She looked down at her wet dress suddenly, as if it had not occurred to her before that it was raining. Then she drew first one little foot and then the other out of the muddy puddle in which she had been standing, and, moving a little closer to the window, said, "I'm not jist goin' home, mem. I'd like to stop here a bit."

So I left her. But, after I had gone a few blocks, the impulse seized me to return by a cross street, and see if she were still there. Tears sprang to my eyes as I first caught sight of the upright little figure, standing in the same spot, still pointing with the rhythmic finger to the blues and reds and yellows, and half chanting under her breath, as before, "I choose *that* color." "I choose *that* color." "I choose *that* color."

I went quietly on my way, without disturbing her again. But I said in my heart, "Little Messenger, Interpreter, Teacher! I will remember you all my life."

Why should days ever be dark, life ever be colorless? There is always sun; there are always blue and scarlet and yellow and purple. We cannot reach them, perhaps, but we can see them, if it is only "through a glass," and "darkly,"—still we can see them. We can "choose" our colors. It rains, perhaps; and we are standing in the cold. Never mind. If we look earnestly enough at the brightness which is on the other side of the glass, we shall forget the wet and not feel the cold. And now and then a passer-by, who has rolled himself up in furs to keep out the cold, but shivers nevertheless,—who has money in his purse to buy many colors, if he likes, but, nevertheless, goes grumbling because some colors are too dear for him,—such a passer-by, chancing to hear our voice, and see the atmosphere of our content, may learn a wondrous secret, — that pennilessness is not poverty, and ownership is not possession; that to be without is not always to lack, and to reach is not to attain; that sunlight is for all eyes that look up, and color for those who "choose."

THE APOSTLE OF BEAUTY.

HE is not of the twelve, any more than the golden rule is of the ten. "A greater commandment I give unto you," was said of that. Also it was called the "new commandment." Yet it was really older than the rest, and greater only because it included them all. There were those who kept it ages before Moses went up Sinai: Joseph, for instance, his ancestor; and the king's daughter, by whose goodness he lived. So stands the Apostle of Beauty, greater than the twelve, newer and older; setting Gospel over against law, having known law before its beginning; living triumphantly free and unconscious of penalty.

He has had martyrdom, and will have. His church is never established; the world does not follow him; only of Wisdom is he known, and of her children, who are children of light. He never speaks by their mouths who say "Shalt not." He knows that "shalt not" is illegitimate, puny, trying always to usurp the throne of the true king, "Thou shalt."

"This is delight," "this is good to see," he says of a purity, of a fair thing. It needs not to speak of the impurity, of the ugliness. Left unmentioned, unforbidden, who knows how soon they might die out of men's lives, perhaps even from the earth's surface? Men hedging gardens have for centuries set plants under that "letter of law" which "killeth," until the very word hedge has become a pain and an offence; and all the while there have been standing in every wild country graceful walls of unhindered brier and berry, to which the apostles of beauty have been silently pointing. By degrees gardeners have learned something. The best of them now call themselves "landscape gardeners;" and that is a concession, if it means, as I suppose it does, that they will try to copy Nature's landscapes in their enclosures. I have seen also of late that on rich men's estates tangled growths of native bushes are being more let alone, and hedges seem to have had some of the weights and harness taken off of them.

This is but one little matter among millions with which the Apostle of Beauty has to do; but it serves for instance of the first requisite he demands, which is freedom. "Let use take care of itself." "It will," he says. "There is no beauty without freedom."

Nothing is too high for him, nothing too low or small. To speak more truly, in his eyes there is no small, no low. From a philanthropy down to a gown, one catholic necessity, one catholic principle; gowns can be benefactions or injuries; philanthropies can be well or ill clad.

He has a ministry of co-workers, — men, women, and guileless little children. Many of them serve him without knowing him by name. Some who serve him best, who spread his creeds most widely, who teach them most eloquently, die without dreaming that they have been missionaries to Gentiles. Others there are who call him "Lord, Lord," build temples to him and teach in them, who never know him. These are they who give their goods to the poor, their bodies to be burned; but are each day ungracious, unloving, hard, cruel to men and women about them. These are they also who make bad statues, bad pictures, invent frightful fashions of things to be worn, and make the houses and the rooms in which they live hideous with unsightly adornments. The centuries fight such, — now with a Titian, a Michel Angelo; now with a great philanthropist, who is also peaceable and easy to be entreated; now with a Florence Nightingale, knowing no sect; now with a little child by a roadside, holding up a marigold in the sun; now with a sweet-faced old woman, dying gracefully in some almshouse. Who has not heard voice from such apostles?

To-day my nearest, most eloquent apostle of beauty is a poor shoemaker, who lives in the house where I lodge. How poor he must be I dare not even try to understand. He has six children: the oldest not more than thirteen, the third a deaf-mute, the baby puny and ill, — sure, I think (and hope), to die soon.

They live in two rooms, on the ground-floor. His shop is the right-hand corner of the front room; the rest is bedroom and sitting-room; behind are the bedroom and kitchen. I have never seen so much as I might of their way of living; for I stand before his window with more reverent fear of intruding by a look than I should have at the door of a king's chamber. A narrow rough ledge added to the window-sill is his bench. Behind this he sits from six in the morning till seven at night, bent over, sewing slowly and painfully on the coarsest shoes. His face looks old enough for sixty years ; but he cannot be so old. Yet he wears glasses and walks feebly; he has probably never had in any one day of his life enough to eat. But I do not know any man, and I know only one woman, who has such a look of radiant good-cheer and content as has this poor shoemaker, Anton Grasl.

In his window are coarse wooden boxes, in which are growing the common mallows. They are just now in full bloom, — row upon row of gay-striped purple and white bells. The window looks to the east, and is never shut. When I go out to my breakfast the sun is streaming in on the flowers and Anton's face. He looks up, smiles, bows low, and says, "Good-day, good my lady," sometimes holding the mallow-stalks back with one hand, to see me more plainly. I feel as if the day and I had had benediction. It is always a better day because Anton has said it is good; and I am a better woman for sight of his godly contentment. Almost every day he has beside the mallows in the boxes a white mug with flowers in it, — nasturtiums, perhaps, or a few pinks. This he sets carefully in shade of the thickest mallows ; and this I have often seen him hold down tenderly, for the little ones to see and to smell.

When I come home in the evenings, between eight and nine o'clock, Anton is always sitting in front of the door, resting his head against the wall. This is his recreation, his one blessed hour of out-door air and rest. He stands with his cap in his hand while I pass, and his face shines as if all the concentrated enjoyment of my walk in the woods had descended upon him in my first look. If I give him a bunch of ferns to add to his nasturtiums and pinks, he is so grateful and delighted that I have to go into the house quickly for fear I shall cry. Whenever I am coming back from a drive, I begin to think, long before I reach the house, how glad Anton will look when he sees the carriage stop. I am as sure as if I had omniscient sight into the depths of his good heart that he has distinct and unenvious joy in every pleasure that he sees other people taking.

Never have I heard one angry or hasty word, one petulant or weary cry from the rooms in which this father and mother and six children are struggling to live. All day long the barefooted and ragged little ones play under my south windows, and do not quarrel. I amuse myself by dropping grapes or plums on their heads, and then watching them at their feast; never have I seen them dispute or struggle in the division. Once I purposely threw a large bunch of grapes to the poor little mute, and only a few plums to the others. I am sorry to say that voiceless Carl ate all his grapes himself; but not a selfish or discontented look could I see on the faces of the others,—they all smiled and beamed up at me like suns.

It is Anton who creates and sustains this rare atmosphere. The wife is only a common and stupid woman; he is educating her, as he is the children. She is very thin and worn and hungry-looking, but always smiles. Being Anton's wife, she could not do otherwise.

Sometimes I see people passing the house, who give a careless glance of contemptuous pity at Anton's window of mallows and nasturtiums. Then I remember that an apostle wrote:—

"There are, it may be, so many kinds of voices in the world, and none of them is without signification.

"Therefore, if I know not the meaning of the voice, I shall be unto him that speaketh a barbarian, and he that speaketh shall be a barbarian unto me."

And I long to call after them, as they go groping their way down the beautiful street,—

"Oh, ye barbarians, blind and deaf! How dare you think you can pity Anton? His soul would melt in compassion for you, if he were able to comprehend that lives could be so poor as yours. He is the rich man, and you are poor. Eating only the husks on which you feed, he would starve to death."

ENGLISH LODGING-HOUSES.

SOMEBODY who has written stories (is it Dickens ?) has given us very wrong ideas of the English lodging-house. What good American does not go into London with the distinct impression that, whatever else he does or does not do, he will upon no account live in lodgings ? That he will even be content with the comfortless coffee-room of a second-rate hotel, and fraternize with commercial travellers from all quarters of the globe, rather than come into relations with that mixture of vulgarity and dishonesty, the lodging-house keeper ?

It was with more than such misgiving that I first crossed the threshold of Mrs. ——'s house in Bedford Place, Bloomsbury. At this distance I smile to remember how welcome would have been any alternative rather than the remaining under her roof for a month ; how persistently for several days I doubted and resisted the evidence of all my senses, and set myself at work to find the discomforts and shortcomings which I believed must belong to that mode of life. To confess the stupidity and obstinacy of my ignorance is small reparation, and would be little worth while, except for the hope that my account of the comfort and economy in living on the English lodging-house system may be a seed dropped in due season, which shall spring up sooner or later in the introduction of a similar system in America. The gain which it would be to great numbers of our men and women who must live on small incomes cannot be estimated. It seems hardly too much to say that in the course of one generation it might work in the average public health a change which would be shown in statistics, and rid us of the stigma of a "national disease" of dyspepsia. For the men and women whose sufferings and ill-health have made of our name a by-word among the nations are not, as many suppose, the rich men and women, tempted by their riches to over-indulgence of their stomachs, and paying in their dyspepsia simply the fair price of their folly; they are the moderately poor men and women, who are paying cruel penalty for not having been richer, — not having been rich enough to avoid the poisons which are cooked and served in American restaurants and in the poorer class of American homes.

Mrs. ——'s lodging-house was not, so far as I know, any better than the average lodging-houses of its grade. It was well situated, well furnished, well kept, and its scale of prices was moderate. For instance, the rent of a pleasant parlor and bedroom on the second floor was thirty-four shillings a week, including fire and gas, — $8.50, gold. Then there was a charge of two shillings a week for the use of the kitchen-fire, and three shillings a week for service; and these were the only charges in addition to the rent. Thus for $9.75 a week one had all the comforts that can be had in housekeeping, so far as room and service are concerned. There were four good servants, — cook, scullery maid, and two housemaids. Oh, the pleasant voices and gentle fashions of behavior of those housemaids! They were slow, it must be owned; but their results were admirable. In spite of London smoke and grime, Mrs. ——'s floors and windows were clean; the grates shone every morning like mirrors, and the glass and silver were bright. Each morning the smiling cook came up to take our orders for the meals of the day; each day the grocer and the baker and the butcher stopped at the door and left the sugar for the "first floor front," the beef for the "drawing-room," and so on. The smallest article which could be required in housekeeping was not overlooked. The groceries of the different floors never got mixed, though how this separateness of stores was accomplished will for ever remain a mystery to me; but that it was successfully accomplished the smallness of our bill was the best of proof, — unless, indeed, as we were sometimes almost afraid, we did now and then eat up Dr. A——'s cheese, or drink the milk belonging to the B's below us. We were a party of four; our fare was of the plain, substantial sort, but of sufficient variety and abundance; and yet our living never cost us, including rent, service, fires, and food, over $60 a week. If we had chosen to practise closer economies, we might have lived on less. Compare for one instant the comfort of such an arrangement as this, which really gave us every possible advantage to be secured by housekeeping, and with almost none of the trouble, with any boarding or lodging possible in New York. We had two parlors and two bedrooms; our meals served promptly and neatly, in our own parlor. The same amount of room, and service, and such a table, for four people, cannot be had in New York for less than $150 or $200 a week; in fact, they cannot be had in New York for any sum of money. The quiet respectfulness of behavior and faithful interest in work of English servants on English soil are not to be found elsewhere. We afterward lived for some weeks in another lodging-house in Great Malvern, Worcestershire, at about the same price per week. This house was even better than the London one in some respects. The system was precisely the same; but the cooking was almost faultless, and the table appointments were more than satisfactory, — they were tasteful. The china was a pleasure, and there were silver and linen and glass which one would be glad to have in one's own home.

It may be asked, and not unnaturally, how does this lodging-house system work for those who keep the houses? Can it be possible that all this comfort and economy for lodgers are compatible with profits for landlords? I can judge only from the results in these two cases which came under my own observation. In each of these cases the family who kept the house lived comfortably and pleasantly in their own apartment, which was, in the London house, almost as good a suite of rooms as any which they rented. They certainly had far more apparent quiet, comfort, and privacy than is commonly seen in the arrangements of the keepers of average boarding-houses. In the Malvern house, one whole floor, which was less pleasant than the others, but still comfortable and well furnished, was occupied by the family. There were three little boys, under ten years of age, who had their nursery governess, said lessons to her regularly, and were led out decorously to walk by her at appointed seasons, like all the rest of good little English boys in well-regulated families ; and yet the mother of these children came to the door of our parlor each morning, with the respectful air of an old family housekeeper, to ask what we would have for dinner, and was careful and exact in buying "three penn'orth" of herbs at a time for us, to season our soup. I ought to mention that in both these places we made the greater part of our purchases ourselves, having weekly bills sent in from the shops, and in our names, exactly as if we were living in our own house. All honest lodging-house keepers, we were told, preferred this method, as leaving no opening for any unjust suspicions of their fairness in providing. But, if one chooses to be as absolutely free from trouble as in boarding, the marketing can all be done by the family, and the bills still made out in the lodgers' names. I have been thus minute in my details because I think there may be many to whom this system of living is as unknown as it was to me ; and I cannot but hope that it may yet be introduced in America.

WET THE CLAY.

ONCE I stood in Miss Hosmer's studio, looking at a statue which she was modelling of the ex-queen of Naples. Face to face with the clay model, I always feel the artist's creative power far more than when I am looking at the immovable marble.

A touch here — there — and all is changed. Perhaps, under my eyes, in the twinkling of an eye, one trait springs into life and another disappears.

The queen, who is a very beautiful woman, was represented in Miss Hosmer's statue as standing, wearing the picturesque cloak that she wore during those hard days of garrison life at Gaeta, when she showed herself so brave and strong that the world said if she, instead of that very stupid young man her husband, had been king, the throne need not have been lost. The very cloak, made of light cloth showily faced with scarlet, was draped over a lay figure in one corner of the room. In the statue the folds of drapery over the right arm were entirely disarranged, simply rough clay. The day before they had been apparently finished; but that morning Miss Hosmer had, as she laughingly told us, "pulled it all to pieces again."

As she said this, she took up a large syringe and

showered the statue from head to foot with water, till it dripped and shone as if it had been just plunged into a bath. Now it was in condition to be moulded. Many times a day this process must be repeated, or the clay becomes so dry and hard that it cannot be worked.

I had known this before ; but never did I so realize the significant symbolism of the act as when I looked at this lifeless yet lifelike thing, to be made into the beauty of a woman, called by her name, and cherished after her death, — and saw that only through this chrysalis of the clay, so cared for, moistened, and moulded, could the marble obtain its soul.

And, as all things I see in life seem to me to have a voice either for or of children, so did this instantly suggest to me that most of the failures of mothers come from their not keeping the clay wet.

The slightest touch tells on the clay when it is soft and moist, and can produce just the effect which is desired; but when the clay is too dry it will not yield, and often it breaks and crumbles beneath the unskilful hand. How perfect the analogy between these two results, and the two atmospheres which one often sees in the space of one half-hour in the management of the same child! One person can win from it instantly a gentle obedience: that person's smile is a reward, that person's displeasure is a grief it cannot bear, that person's opinions have utmost weight with it, that person's presence is a controlling and subduing influence. Another, alas! the mother, produces such an opposite effect that it is hard to believe the child can be the same child. Her simplest command is met by antagonism or sullen compliance; her pleasure and displeasure are plainly of no account to the child, and its great desire is to get out of her presence.

What shape will she make of that child's soul? She does not wet the clay. She does not stop to consider before each command whether it be wholly just, whether it be the best time to make it, and whether she can explain its necessity. Oh! the sweet reasonableness of children when disagreeable necessities are explained to them, instead of being enforced as arbitrary tyrannies! She does not make them so feel that she shares all their sorrows and pleasures that they cannot help being in turn glad when she is glad, and sorry when she is sorry. She does not so take them into constant companionship in her interests, each day, — the books, the papers she reads, the things she sees, — that they learn to hold her as the representative of much more than nursery discipline, clothes, and bread and butter. She does not kiss them often enough, put her arms around them, warm, soften, bathe them in the ineffable sunshine of loving ways. "I can't imagine why children are so much better with you than with me," exclaims such a mother. No, she cannot imagine; and that is the trouble. If she could, all would be righted. It is quite probable that she is a far more anxious, self-sacrificing, hard-working mother than the neighbor, whose children are rosy and frolicking and affectionate and obedient; while hers are pale and fretful and selfish and sullen.

She is all the time working, working, with endless activity, on hard, dry clay; and the neighbor, who, perhaps half-unconsciously, keeps the clay wet, is with one-half the labor modelling sweet creatures of Nature's own loveliest shapes.

Then she says, this poor, tired mother, discouraged because her children tell lies, and irritated because they seem to her thankless, "After all, children are pretty much alike, I suppose. I believe most children tell lies when they are little; and they never realize until they are grown up what parents do for them."

Here again I find a similitude among the artists who paint or model. Studios are full of such caricatures, and the hard-working, honest souls who have made them believe that they are true reproductions of nature and life.

"See my cherub. Are not all cherubs such as he?" and "Behold these trees and this water; and how the sun glowed on the day when I walked there!" and all the while the cherub is like a paper doll, and the trees and the water never had any likeness to any thing that is in this beautiful earth. But, after all, this similitude is short and paltry, for it is of comparatively small moment that so many men and women spend their lives in making bad cherubs in marble, and hideous landscapes in oil. It is industry, and it keeps them in bread; in butter, too, if their cherubs and trees are very bad. But, when it is a human being that is to be moulded, how do we dare, even with all the help which we can ask and find in earth and in heaven, to shape it by our touch!

Clay in the hands of the potter is not more plastic than is the little child's soul in the hands of those who tend it. Alas ! how many shapeless, how many ill-formed, how many broken do we see ! Who does not believe that the image of God could have been beautiful on all ? Sooner or later it will be, thank Christ ! But what a pity, what a loss, not to have had the sweet blessedness of being even here fellow-workers with him in this glorious modelling for eternity !

THE KING'S FRIEND.

WE are a gay party, summering among the hills. New-comers into the little boarding-house where we, by reason of prior possession, hold a kind of sway are apt to fare hardly at our hands unless they come up to our standard. We are not exacting in the matter of clothes; we are liberal on creeds; but we have our shibboleths. And, though we do not drown unlucky Ephraimites, whose tongues make bad work with S's, I fear we are not quite kind to them; they never stay long, and so we go on having it much our own way.

Week before last a man appeared at dinner, of whom our good little landlady said, deprecatingly, that he would stay only a few days. She knew by instinct that his presence would not be agreeable to us. He was not in the least an intrusive person, — on the contrary, there was a sort of mute appeal to our humanity in the very extent of his quiet inoffensiveness; but his whole atmosphere was utterly uninteresting. He was untrained in manner, awkwardly ill at ease in the table routine; and, altogether, it was so uncomfortable to make any attempt to include him in our circle that in a few days he was ignored by every one, to a degree which was neither courteous nor Christian.

In all families there is a leader. Ours is a charming and brilliant married woman, whose ready wit and never-failing spirits make her the best of centres for a country party of pleasure-seekers. Her keen sense of humor had not been able entirely to spare this unfortunate man, whose attitudes and movements were certainly at times almost irresistible.

But one morning such a change was apparent in her manner toward him that we all looked up in surprise. No more gracious and gentle greeting could she have given him if he had been a prince of royal line. Our astonishment almost passed bounds when we heard her continue with a kindly inquiry after his health, and, undeterred by his evident readiness to launch into detailed symptoms, listen to him with the most respectful attention. Under the influence of this new and sweet recognition his plain and common face kindled into something almost manly and individual. He had never before been so spoken to by a well-bred and beautiful woman.

We were sobered, in spite of ourselves, by an indefinable something in her manner; and it was with subdued whispers that we crowded around her on the piazza, and begged to know what it all meant. It was a rare thing to see Mrs. —— hesitate for a reply. The color rose in her face, and, with a half-nervous attempt at a smile, she finally said, "Well, girls, I suppose you will all laugh at me; but the truth is, I heard that man say his prayers this morning. You know his room is next to mine, and there is a great crack in the door. I heard him praying, this morning, for ten minutes, just before breakfast; and I never heard such tones in my life. I don't pretend to be religious ; but I must own it was a wonderful thing to hear a man talking with God as he did. And when I saw him at table, I felt as if I were looking in the face of some one who had just come out of the presence of the King of kings, and had the very air of heaven about him. I can't help what the rest of you do or say ; *I* shall always have the same feeling whenever I see him."

There was a magnetic earnestness in her tone and look, which we all felt, and which some of us will never forget.

During the few remaining days of his stay with us, that untutored, uninteresting, stupid man knew no lack of friendly courtesy at our hands. We were the better for his homely presence ; unawares, he ministered unto us. When we knew that he came directly from speaking to the Master to speak to us, we felt that he was greater than we, and we remembered that it is written, " If any man serve me, him will my Father honor."

LEARNING TO SPEAK.

WITH what breathless interest we listen for the baby's first word! What a new bond is at once and for ever established between its soul and ours by this mysterious, inexplicable, almost incredible fact! That is the use of the word. That is its only use, so far as mere gratification of the ear goes. Many other sounds are more pleasurable, — the baby's laugh, for instance, or its inarticulate murmurs of content or sleepiness.

But the word is a revelation, a sacred sign. Now we shall know what our beloved one wants; now we shall know when and why the dear heart sorrows or is glad. How reassured we feel, how confident! Now we cannot make mistakes; we shall do all for the best; we can give happiness; we can communicate wisdom; relation is established; the perplexing gulf of silence is bridged. The baby speaks!

But it is not of the baby's learning to speak that we propose to write here. All babies learn to speak; or, if they do not, we know that it means a terrible visitation, — a calamity rare, thank God! but bitter almost beyond parents' strength to bear.

But why, having once learned to speak, does the

baby leave off speaking when it becomes a man or a woman? Many of our men and women to-day need, almost as much as when they were twenty-four months old, to learn to speak. We do not mean learning to speak in public. We do not mean even learning to speak well, — to pronounce words clearly and accurately; though there is need enough of that in this land! But that is not the need at which we are aiming now. We mean something so much simpler, so much further back, that we hardly know how to say it in words which shall be simple enough and also sufficiently strong. We mean learning to speak at all! In spite of all which satirical writers have said and say of the loquacious egotism, the questioning curiosity of our people, it is true to-day that the average American is a reticent, taciturn, speechless creature, who, for his own sake, and still more for the sake of all who love him, needs, more than he needs any thing else under heaven, to learn to speak.

Look at our silent railway and horse-cars, steamboat-cabins, hotel-tables, in short, all our public places where people are thrown together incidentally, and where good-will and the habit of speaking combined would create an atmosphere of human vitality, quite unlike what we see now. But it is not of so much consequence, after all, whether people speak in these public places or not. If they did, one very unpleasant phase of our national life would be greatly changed for the better. But it is in our homes that this speechlessness tells most fearfully, — on the breakfast and dinner and tea-tables, at which a silent father and mother sit down in haste and gloom to feed their depressed children. This is especially true of men and women in the rural districts. They are tired; they have more work to do in a year than it is easy to do. Their lives are monotonous, — too much so for the best health of either mind or body. If they dreamed how much this monotony could be broken and cheered by the constant habit of talking with each other, they would grasp at the slightest chance of a conversation. Sometimes it almost seems as if complaints and antagonism were better than such stagnant quiet. But there need not be complaint and antagonism; there is no home so poor, so remote from affairs, that each day does not bring and set ready, for family welcome and discussion, beautiful sights and sounds, occasions for helpfulness and gratitude, questions for decision, hopes, fears, regrets! The elements of human life are the same for ever; any one heart holds in itself the whole, can give all things to another, can bear all things for another; but no giving, no bearing, no, not even if it is the giving up of a life, if it is done without free, full, loving interchange of speech, is half the blessing it might be.

Many a wife goes down to her grave a dulled and dispirited woman simply because her good and faithful husband has lived by her side without talking to her! There have been days when one word of praise, or one word even of simple good cheer, would have girded her up with new strength. She did not know, very likely, what she needed, or that she needed any thing; but she drooped.

Many a child grows up a hard, unimpressionable, unloving man or woman simply from the uncheered silence in which the first ten years of life were passed. Very few fathers and mothers, even those who are fluent, perhaps, in society, habitually *talk* with their children.

It is certain that this is one of the worst shortcomings of our homes. Perhaps no other single change would do so much to make them happier, and, therefore, to make our communities better, as for men and women to learn to speak.

PRIVATE TYRANTS.

WE recognize tyranny when it wears a crown and sits on an hereditary throne. We sympathize with nations that overthrow the thrones, and in our secret hearts we almost canonize individuals who slay the tyrants. From the days of Ehud and Eglon down to those of Charlotte Corday and Marat, the world has dealt tenderly with their names whose hands have been red with the blood of oppressors. On moral grounds it would be hard to justify this sentiment, murder being murder all the same, however great gain it may be to this world to have the murdered man put out of it; but that there is such a sentiment, instinctive and strong in the human soul, there is no denying. It is so instinctive and so strong that, if we watch ourselves closely, we shall find it giving alarming shape sometimes to our secret thoughts about our neighbors.

How many communities, how many households even, are without a tyrant? If we could "move for returns of suffering," as that tender and thoughtful man, Arthur Helps, says, we should find a far heavier aggregate of misery inflicted by unsuspected, unresisted tyrannies than by those which are patent to everybody, and sure to be overthrown sooner or later.

An exhaustive sermon on this subject should be set off in three divisions, as follows: —

PRIVATE TYRANTS.

1*st.* Number of—
2*d.* Nature of—
3*d.* Longevity of—

First. Their number. They are not enumerated in any census. Not even the most painstaking statistician has meddled with the topic. Fancy takes bold leaps at the very suggestion of such an estimate, and begins to think at once of all things in the universe which are usually mentioned as beyond numbering. Probably one good way of getting at a certain sort of result would be to ask each person of one's acquaintance, "Do you happen to know a private tyrant?"

How well we know beforehand the replies we should get from *some* beloved men and women, — that is, if they spoke the truth!

But they would not. That is the saddest thing about these private tyrannies. They are in many cases borne in such divine and uncomplaining silence by their victims, perhaps for long years, the world never dreams that they exist. But at last the fine, subtle writing, which no control, no patience, no will can thwart, becomes set on the man's or the woman's face, and tells the whole record. Who does not know such faces? Cheerful usually, even gay, brave, and ready with lines of smile; but in repose so marked, so scarred with unutterable weariness and disappointment, that tears spring in the eyes and love in the hearts of all finely organized persons who meet them.

Secondly. Nature of private tyrants. Here also the statistician has not entered. The field is vast; the analysis difficult.

Selfishness is, of course, their leading characteristic; in fact, the very sum and substance of their natures. But selfishness is Protean. It has as many shapes as there are minutes, and as many excuses and wraps of sheep's clothing as ever ravening wolf possessed.

One of its commonest pleas is that of weakness. Here it often is so inextricably mixed with genuine need and legitimate claim that one grows bewildered between sympathy and resentment. In this shape, however, it gets its cruelest dominion over strong and generous and tender people. This kind of tyranny builds up and fortifies its bulwarks on and out of the very virtues of its victims; it gains strength hourly from the very strength of the strength to which it appeals; each slow and fatal encroachment never seems at first so much a thing required as a thing offered; but, like the slow sinking inch by inch of that great, beautiful city of stone into the relentless Adriatic, so is the slow, sure going down and loss of the freedom of a strong, beautiful soul, helpless in the omnipresent circumference of the selfish nature to which it is or believes itself bound.

That the exactions never or rarely take shape in words is, to the unbiassed looker-on, only an exasperating feature in their tyranny. While it saves the conscience of the tyrant, — if such tyrants have any, — it makes doubly sure the success of their tyranny. And probably nothing short of revelation from Heaven, in shape of blinding light, would ever open their eyes to the fact that it is even more selfish to hold a generous spirit fettered hour by hour by a constant fear of giving pain than to coerce or threaten or scold them into the desired behavior. Invalids, all invalids, stand in deadly peril of becoming tyrants of this order. A chronic invalid who entirely escapes it must be so nearly saint or angel that one instinctively feels as if their invalidism would soon end in the health of heaven. We know of one invalid woman, chained to her bed for long years by an incurable disease, who has had the insight and strength to rise triumphant above this danger. Her constant wish and entreaty is that her husband should go freely into all the work and the pleasure of life. Whenever he leaves her, her farewell is not, "How soon do you think you shall come back? At what hour, or day, may I look for you?" but, "Now, pray stay just as long as you enjoy it. If you hurry home one hour sooner for the thought of me, I shall be wretched." It really seems almost as if the longer he stayed away, — hours, days, weeks even, — the happier she were.

By this sweet and wise unselfishness she has succeeded in realizing the whole blessedness of wifehood far more than most women who have health. But we doubt if any century sees more than one such woman as she is.

Another large class, next to that of invalids the most difficult to deal with, is made up of people who are by nature or by habit uncomfortably sensitive or irritable. Who has not lived at one time or other in his life in daily contact with people of this sort, — persons whose outbreaks of temper, or of wounded feeling still worse than temper, were as incalculable as meteoric showers? The suppressed atmosphere, the chronic state of alarm and misgiving, in which the victims of this species of tyranny live are withering and exhausting to the stoutest hearts. They are also hardening; perpetually having to wonder and watch how people will "take" things is apt sooner or later to result in indifference as to whether they take them well or ill.

But to define all the shapes of private tyranny would require whole histories; it is safe, however, to say that so far as any human being attempts to set up his own individual need or preference as law to determine the action of any other human being, in small matters or great, so far forth he is a tyrant. The limit of his tyranny may be narrowed by lack of power on his part, or of response on the part of his fellows; but its essence is as purely tyrannous as if he sat on a throne with an executioner within call.

Thirdly. Longevity of private tyrants. We have

not room under this head to do more — nor, if we had all room, could we do better — than to quote a short paragraph from George Eliot's immortal Mrs. Poyser: "It seems as if them as aren't wanted here are th' only folks as aren't wanted i' th' other world."

MARGIN.

WIDE-MARGINED pages please us at first sight. We do not stop to ask why. It has passed into an accepted rule that all elegant books must have broad, clear margins to their pages. We as much recognize such margins among the indications of promise in a book, as we do fineness of paper, clearness of type, and beauty of binding. All three of these last, even in perfection, could not make any book beautiful, or sightly, whose pages had been left narrow-margined and crowded. This is no arbitrary decree of custom, no chance preference of an accredited authority. It would be dangerous to set limit to the power of fashion in any thing; and yet it seems almost safe to say that not even fashion itself can ever make a narrow-margined page look other than shabby and mean. This inalienable right of the broad margin to our esteem is significant. It lies deep. The broad margin means something which is not measured by inches, has nothing to do with fashions of shape. It means room for notes, queries, added by any man's hand who reads. Meaning this, it means also much more than this, — far more than the mere letter of "right of way." It is a fine courtesy of recognition that no one page shall ever say the whole of its own message; be exhaustive, or ultimate, even of its own topic; determine or enforce its own opinion, to the shutting out of others. No matter if the book live and grow old, without so much as an interrogation point or a line of enthusiastic admiration drawn in it by human hand, still the gracious import and suggestion of its broad white spaces are the same. Each thought invites its neighbor, stands fairly to right or left of its opponent, and wooes its friend.

Thinking on this, we presently discover that margin means a species of freedom. No wonder the word, and the thing it represents, wherever we find them, delight us.

We use the word constantly in senses which, speaking carelessly, we should have called secondary and borrowed. Now we see that its application to pages, or pictures, or decorations, and so forth, was the borrowed and secondary use; and that primarily its meaning is spiritual.

We must have margin, or be uncomfortable in every thing in life. Our plan for a day, for a week, for our lifetime, must have it, — margin for change of purpose, margin for interruption, margin for accident. Making no allowance for these, we are fettered, we are disturbed, we are thwarted.

Is there a greater misery than to be hurried? If we leave ourselves proper margin, we never need to be hurried. We always shall be, if we crowd our plan. People pant, groan, and complain as if hurry were a thing outside of themselves, — an enemy, a monster, a disease which overtook them, and against which they had no shelter. It is hard to be patient with such nonsense. Hurry is almost the only known misery which it is impossible to have brought upon one by other people's fault.

If our plan of action for an hour or a day be so fatally spoiled by lack of margin, what shall we say of the mistake of the man who leaves himself no margin in matters of belief? No room for a wholesome, healthy doubt? No provision for an added enlightenment? No calculation for the inevitable progress of human knowledge? This is, in our eyes, the crying sin and danger of elaborate creeds, rigid formulas of exact statement on difficult and hidden mysteries.

The man who is ready to give pledge that the opinion he will hold to-morrow will be precisely the opinion he holds to-day has either thought very little, or to little purpose, or has resolved to quit thinking altogether.

THE FINE ART OF SMILING.

SOME theatrical experiments are being made at this time to show that all possible emotions and all shades and gradations of emotion can be expressed by facial action, and that the method of so expressing them can be reduced to a system, and taught in a given number of lessons. It seems a matter of question whether one would be likely to make love or evince sorrow any more successfully by keeping in mind all the while the detailed catalogue of his flexors and extensors, and contracting and relaxing No. 1, 2, or 3, according to rule. The human memory is a treacherous thing, and what an enormous disaster would result from a very slight forgetfulness in such a nicely adjusted system! The fatal effect of dropping the superior maxillary when one intended to drop the inferior, or of applying nervous stimuli to the up track, instead of the down, can easily be conceived. Art is art, after all, be it ever so skilful and triumphant, and science is only a slow reading of hieroglyphs. Nature sits high and serene above both, and smiles compassionately on their efforts to imitate and understand. And this brings us to what we have to say about smiling. Do many people feel what a wonderful thing it is that each human being is born into the world with his own smile? Eyes, nose, mouth, may be merely average commonplace features; may look, taken singly, very much like anybody's else eyes, nose, or mouth. Let whoever doubts this try the simple but endlessly amusing experiment of setting half a dozen people behind a perforated curtain, and making them put their eyes at the holes. Not one eye in a hundred can be recognized, even by most familiar and loving friends. But study smiles; observe, even in the most casual way, the variety one sees in a day, and it will soon be felt what subtle revelation they make, what infinite individuality they possess.

The purely natural smile, however, is seldom seen in adults; and it is on this point that we wish to dwell. Very early in life people find out that a smile is a weapon, mighty to avail in all sorts of crises. Hence, we see the treacherous smile of the wily; the patronizing smile of the pompous; the obsequious smile of the flatterer; the cynical smile of the satirist. Very few of these have heard of Delsarte; but they outdo him on his own grounds. Their smile is four-fifths of their social stock in trade. All such smiles are hideous. The gloomiest, blankest look which a human face can wear is welcomer than a trained smile or a smile which, if it is not actually and consciously methodized by its perpetrator, has become, by long repetition, so associated with tricks and falsities that it partakes of their quality.

What, then, is the fine art of smiling?

If smiles may not be used for weapons or masks, of what use are they? That is the shape one would think the question took in most men's minds, if we may judge by their behavior! There are but two legitimate purposes of the smile; but two honest smiles. On all little children's faces such smiles are seen. Woe to us that we so soon waste and lose them!

The first use of the smile is to express affectionate good-will; the second, to express mirth.

Why do we not always smile whenever we meet the eye of a fellow-being? That is the true, intended recognition which ought to pass from soul to soul constantly. Little children, in simple communities, do this involuntarily, unconsciously. The honest-hearted German peasant does it. It is like magical sunlight all through that simple land, the perpetual greeting on the right hand and on the left, between strangers, as they pass by each other, never without a smile. This, then, is "the fine art of smiling;" like all fine art, true art, perfection of art, the simplest following of Nature.

Now and then one sees a face which has kept its smile pure and undefiled. It is a woman's face usually; often a face which has trace of great sorrow all over it, till the smile breaks. Such a smile transfigures; such a smile, if the artful but knew it, is the greatest weapon a face can have. Sickness and age cannot turn its edge; hostility and distrust cannot withstand its spell; little children know it, and smile back; even dumb animals come closer, and look up for another.

If one were asked to sum up in one single rule what would most conduce to beauty in the human face, one might say therefore, "Never tamper with your smile; never once use it for a purpose. Let it be on your face like the reflection of the sunlight on a lake. Affectionate good-will to all men must be the sunlight, and your face is the lake. But, unlike the sunlight, your good-will must be perpetual, and your face must never be overcast."

"What! smile perpetually?" says the realist. "How silly!"

Yes, smile perpetually! Go to Delsarte here, and learn even from the mechanician of smiles that a smile can be indicated by a movement of muscles so slight that neither instruments nor terms exist to measure or state it; in fact, that the subtlest smile is little more than an added brightness to the eye and a tremulousness of the mouth. One second of time is more than long enough for it; but eternity does not outlast it.

In that wonderfully wise and tender and poetic book, the "Layman's Breviary," Leopold Schefer says, —

"A smile suffices to smile death away;
And love defends thee e'en from wrath divine!
Then let what may befall thee, — still smile on!
And howe'er Death may rob thee, — still smile on!
Love never has to meet a bitter thing;
A paradise blooms around him who smiles."

DEATH-BED REPENTANCE.

NOT long since, a Congregationalist clergyman, who had been for forty-one years in the ministry, said in my hearing, "I have never, in all my experience as a pastor, known of a single instance in which a repentance on what was supposed to be a death-bed proved to be of any value whatever after the person recovered."

This was strong language. I involuntarily exclaimed, "Have you known many such cases?"

"More than I dare to remember."

"And as many more, perhaps, where the person died."

"Yes, fully as many more.

"Then did not the bitter failure of these death-bed repentances to bear the tests of time shake your confidence in their value under the tests of eternity?"

"It did, — it does," said the clergyman, with tears in his eyes. The conversation made a deep impression on my mind. It was strong evidence, from a quarter in which I least looked for it, of the utter paltriness and insufficiency of fear as a motive when brought to bear upon decisions in spiritual things. There seem to be no words strong enough to stigmatize it in all other affairs except spiritual. All ages, all races, hold cowardice chief among vices; noble barbarians punished it with death. Even civilization the most cautiously legislated for, does the same thing when a soldier shows it "in face of the enemy." Language, gathering itself up and concentrating its force to describe base behavior, can do no more than call it "cowardly." No instinct of all the blessed body-guard of instincts born with us seems in the outset a stronger one than the instinct that to be noble, one must be brave. Almost in the cradle the baby taunts or is taunted by the accusation of being "afraid." And the sting of the taunt lies in the probability of its truth. For in all men, alas! is born a certain selfish weakness, to which fear can address itself. But how strange does it appear that they who wish to inculcate noblest action, raise to most exalted spiritual conditions, should appeal to this lowest of motives to help them! We believe that there are many "death-bed repentances" among hale, hearty sinners, who are approached by the same methods, stimulated by the same considerations, frightened by the same conceptions of possible future suffering, which so often make the chambers of dying men dark with terrors. Fear is fear all the same whether its dread be for the next hour or the next century. The closer the enemy, the swifter it runs. That is all the difference. Let the enemy be surely and plainly removed, and in one instance it is no more, — is as if it had never been. Every thought, word, and action based upon it has come to end.

I was forcibly reminded of the conversation above quoted by some observations I once had opportunity of making at a Methodist camp-meeting. Much of the preaching and exhortation consisted simply and solely of urgent, impassioned appeals to the people to repent, — not because repentance is right; not because God is love, and it is base not to love and obey him; not even because godliness is in itself great gain, and sinfulness is, even temporarily, loss and ruin; but because there is a wrath to come, which will inflict terrible and unending suffering on the sinner. He is to "flee" for his life from torments indescribable and eternal; he is to call on Jesus, not to make him holy, but to save him from woe, to rescue him from frightful danger; all and every thing else is subordinate to the one selfish idea of escaping future misery. The effect of these appeals, of these harrowing pictures, on some of the young men and women and children was almost too painful to be borne. They were in an hysterical condition, — weeping from sheer nervous terror. When the excitement had reached its highest pitch, an elder rose and told the story of a wicked and impenitent man whom he had visited a few weeks before. The man had assented to all that he told him of the necessity of repentance; but said that he was not at leisure that day to attend the class meeting. He resolved and promised, however, to do so the next week. That very night he was taken ill with a disease of the brain, and, after three days of unconsciousness, died. I would not like to quote here the emphasis of application which was made of this story to the terrors of the weeping young people. Under its influence several were led, almost carried by force, into the anxious seats.

It was hard not to fancy the gentle Christ looking down upon the scene with a pain as great as that with which he yearned over Jerusalem. I longed for some instant miracle to be wrought on the spot, by which there should come floating down from the peaceful blue sky, through the sweet tree-tops, some of the loving and serene words of balm from his Gospel.

Theologians may theorize, and good Christians may differ (they always will) as to the existence, extent, and nature of future punishment; but the fact remains indisputably clear that, whether there be less or more of it, whether it be of this sort or of that, fear of it is a base motive to appeal to, a false motive to act from, and a worthless motive to trust in. Perfect love does not know it; spiritual courage resents it; the true Kingdom of Heaven is never taken by its "violence."

Somewhere (I wish I knew where, and I wish I knew from whose lips) I once found this immortal sentence: "A woman went through the streets of Alexandria, bearing a jar of water and a lighted torch, and crying aloud, 'With this torch I will burn up Heaven, and with this water I will put out Hell, that God may be loved for himself alone.'"

THE CORRELATION OF MORAL FORCES.

SCIENCE has dealt and delved patiently with the laws of matter. From Cuvier to Huxley, we have a long line of clear-eyed workers. The gravitating force between all molecules; the law of continuity; the inertial force of matter; the sublime facts of organic co-ordination and adaptation, — all these are recognized, analyzed, recorded, taught. We have learned that the true meaning of the word law, as applied to Nature, is not decree, but formula of invariable order, immutable as the constitution of ultimate units of matter. Order is not imposed upon Nature. Order is result. Physical science does not confuse these; it never mistakes nor denies specific function, organic progression, cyclical growth. It knows that there is no such thing as evasion, interruption, substitution.

When shall we have a Cuvier, a Huxley, a Tyndall for the immaterial world, — the realm of spiritual existence, moral growth? Nature is one. The things which we have clumsily and impertinently dared to set off by themselves, and label as "immaterial," are no less truly component parts or members of the real frame of natural existence than are molecules of oxygen or crystals of diamond. We believe in the existence of one as much as in the existence of the other. In fact, if there be balance of proof in favor of either, it is not in favor of the existence of what we call matter. All the known sensible qualities of matter are ultimately referable to immaterial forces, — "forces acting from points or volumes;" and whether these points are occupied by positive substance, or "matter" as it is usually conceived, cannot to-day be proved. Yet many men have less absolute belief in a soul than in nitric acid; many men achieve lifetimes of triumph by the faithful use and application of Nature's law — that is, formula of uniform occurrence — in light, sound, motion, while they all the while outrage and violate and hinder every one of those sweet forces equally hers, equally immutable, called by such names as truth, sobriety, chastity, courage, and good-will.

The suggestions of this train of thought are too numerous to be followed out in the limits of a single article. Take, for instance, the fact of the identity of molecules, and look for its correlative truth in the spiritual universe. Shall we not thence learn charity, and the better understand the full meaning of some who have said that vices were virtues in excess or restraint? Taking the lists of each, and faithfully comparing them from beginning to end, not one shall be found which will not confirm this seemingly paradoxical statement.

Take the great fact of continuous progressive development which applies to all organisms, vegetable or animal, and see how it is one with the law that "the holy shall be holy still, the wicked shall be wicked still."

Dare we think what would be the formula in statement of spiritual life which would be correlative to the "law of continuity"? Having dared to think, then shall we use the expression "little sins," or doubt the terrible absoluteness of exactitude with which "every idle word which men speak" shall enter upon eternity of reckoning.

On the other hand, looking at all existences as organisms, shall we be disturbed at seeming failure?—long periods of apparent inactivity? Shall we believe, for instance, that Christ's great church can be really hindered in its appropriate cycle of progressive change and adaptation? That any true membership of this organic body can be formed or annulled by mere human interference? That the lopping or burning of branches of the tree, even the uprooting and burning of the tree itself, this year, next year, nay, for hundreds of years, shall have power to annihilate or even defer the ultimate organic result?

The soul of man is not outcast from this glory, this freedom, this safety of law. We speak as if we might break it, evade it; we forget it; we deny it: but it never forgets us, it never refuses us a morsel of our estate. In spite of us, it protects our growth, makes sure of our development. In spite of us, it takes us whithersoever we tend, and not whithersoever we like; in spite of us, it sometimes saves what we have carelessly perilled, and always destroys what we wilfully throw away.

A SIMPLE BILL OF FARE FOR A CHRISTMAS DINNER.

ALL good recipe-books give bills of fare for different occasions, bills of fare for grand dinners, bills of fare for little dinners ; dinners to cost so much per head ; dinners "which can be easily prepared with one servant," and so on. They give bills of fare for one week ; bills of fare for each day in a month, to avoid too great monotony in diet. There are bills of fare for dyspeptics ; bills of fare for consumptives ; bills of fare for fat people, and bills of fare for thin ; and bills of fare for hospitals, asylums, and prisons, as well as for gentlemen's houses. But among them all, we never saw the one which we give below. It has never been printed in any book ; but it has been used in families. We are not drawing on our imagination for its items. We have sat at such dinners ; we have helped prepare such dinners ; we believe in such dinners ; they are within everybody's means. In fact, the most marvellous thing about this bill of fare is that the dinner does not cost a cent. Ho! all ye that are hungry and thirsty, and would like so cheap a Christmas dinner, listen to this

BILL OF FARE FOR A CHRISTMAS DINNER.

First Course. — GLADNESS.

This must be served hot. No two housekeepers make it alike; no fixed rule can be given for it. It depends, like so many of the best things, chiefly on memory; but, strangely enough, it depends quite as much on proper forgetting as on proper remembering. Worries must be forgotten. Troubles must be forgotten. Yes, even sorrow itself must be denied and shut out. Perhaps this is not quite possible. Ah! we all have seen Christmas days on which sorrow would not leave our hearts nor our houses. But even sorrow can be compelled to look away from its sorrowing for a festival hour which is so solemnly joyous as Christ's Birthday. Memory can be filled full of other things to be remembered. No soul is entirely destitute of blessings, absolutely without comfort. Perhaps we have but one. Very well; we can think steadily of that one, if we try. But the probability is that we have more than we can count. No man has yet numbered the blessings, the mercies, the joys of God. We are all richer than we think; and if we once set ourselves to reckoning up the things of which we are glad, we shall be astonished at their number.

Gladness, then, is the first item, the first course on our bill of fare for a Christmas dinner.

Entrées. — LOVE garnished with Smiles.

GENTLENESS, with sweet-wine sauce of Laughter.

GRACIOUS SPEECH, cooked with any fine, savory herbs, such as Drollery, which is always in season, or Pleasant Reminiscence, which no one need be without, as it keeps for years, sealed or unsealed.

Second Course. — HOSPITALITY.

The precise form of this also depends on individual preferences. We are not undertaking here to give exact recipes, only a bill of fare.

In some houses Hospitality is brought on surrounded with Relatives. This is very well. In others, it is dished up with Dignitaries of all sorts; men and women of position and estate for whom the host has special likings or uses. This gives a fine effect to the eye, but cools quickly, and is not in the long-run satisfying.

In a third class, best of all, it is served in simple shapes, but with a great variety of Unfortunate Persons, — such as lonely people from lodging-houses, poor people of all grades, widows and childless in their affliction. This is the kind most preferred; in fact, never abandoned by those who have tried it.

For Dessert. — MIRTH, in glasses.

GRATITUDE and FAITH beaten together and piled up in snowy shapes. These will look light if run over night in the moulds of Solid Trust and Patience.

A dish of the bonbons Good Cheer and Kindliness with every-day mottoes; Knots and Reasons in shape of Puzzles and Answers; the whole ornamented with Apples of Gold in Pictures of Silver, of the kind mentioned in the Book of Proverbs.

This is a short and simple bill of fare. There is not a costly thing in it; not a thing which cannot be procured without difficulty.

If meat is desired, it can be added. That is another excellence about our bill of fare. It has nothing in it which makes it incongruous with the richest or the plainest tables. It is not overcrowded by the addition of roast goose and plum-pudding; it is not harmed by the addition of herring and potatoes. Nay, it can give flavor and richness to broken bits of stale bread served on a doorstep and eaten by beggars.

We might say much more about this bill of fare. We might, perhaps, confess that it has an element of the supernatural; that its origin is lost in obscurity; that, although, as we said, it has never been printed before, it has been known in all ages; that the martyrs feasted upon it; that generations of the poor, called blessed by Christ, have laid out banquets by it; that exiles and prisoners have lived on it; and the despised and forsaken and rejected in all countries have tasted it. It is also true that when any great king ate well and throve on his dinner, it was by the same magic food. The young and the free and the glad, and all rich men in costly houses, even they have not been well fed without it.

And though we have called it a Bill of Fare for a Christmas Dinner, that is only that men's eyes may be caught by its name, and that they, thinking it a specialty for festival, may learn and understand its secret, and henceforth, laying all their dinners according to its magic order, may "eat unto the Lord."

CHILDREN'S PARTIES.

"FROM six till half-past eleven."

"German at seven, precisely."

These were the terms of an invitation which we saw last week. It was sent to forty children, between the ages of ten and sixteen.

"Will you allow your children to stay at this party until half-past eleven?" we said to a mother whose children were invited. "What can I do?" she replied. "If I send the carriage for them at half-past ten, the chances are that they will not be allowed to come away. It is impossible to break up a set. And as for that matter, half-past ten is two hours and a half past their bed-time; they might as well stay an hour longer. I wish nobody would ever ask my children to a party. I cannot keep them at home, if they are asked. Of course, I *might;* but I have not the moral courage to see them so unhappy. All the other children go; and what can I do?"

This is a tender, loving mother, whose sweet, gentle, natural methods with her children have made them sweet, gentle, natural little girls, whom it is a delight to know. But "what can she do?" The question is by no means one which can be readily answered. It is very easy for off-hand severity, sweeping condemnation, to say, "Do! Why, nothing is plainer. Keep her children away from such places. Never let them go to any parties which will last later than nine o'clock." This is the same thing as saying, "Never let them go to parties at all." There are no parties which break up at nine o'clock; that is, there are not in our cities. We hope there are such parties still in country towns and villages,—such parties as we remember to this day with a vividness which no social enjoyments since then have dimmed; Saturday-afternoon parties, — *matinées* they would have been called if the village people had known enough; parties which began at three in the afternoon and ended in the early dusk, while little ones could see their way home; parties at which there was no "German," only the simplest of dancing, if any, and much more of blind-man's-buff; parties at which "mottoes" in sugar horns were the luxurious novelty, caraway cookies the staple, and lemonade the only drink besides pure water. Fancy offering to the creature called child in cities to-day, lemonade and a caraway cooky and a few pink sugar horns and some walnuts and raisins to carry home in its pocket! One blushes at thought of the scornful contempt with which such simples would be received, — we mean rejected!

From the party whose invitation we have quoted above the little girls came home at midnight, radiant, flushed, joyous, looking in their floating white muslin dresses like fairies, their hands loaded with bouquets of hot-house flowers and dainty little "favors" from the German. At eleven they had had for supper champagne and chicken salad, and all the other unwholesome abominations which are set out and eaten in American evening entertainments.

Next morning there were no languid eyes, pale cheeks. Each little face was eager, bright, rosy, though the excited brain had had only five or six hours of sleep.

"If they only would feel tired the next day, that would be something of an argument to bring up with them," said the poor mother. "But they always declare that they feel better than ever."

And so they do. But the "better" is only a deceitful sham, kept up by excited and overwrought nerves,—the same thing that we see over and over and over again in all lives which are temporarily kindled and stimulated by excitement of any kind.

This is the worst thing, this is the most fatal thing in all our mismanagements and perversions of the physical life of our children. Their beautiful elasticity and strength rebound instantly to an apparently uninjured fulness; and so we go on, undermining, undermining at point after point, until suddenly some day there comes a tragedy, a catastrophe, for which we are as unprepared as if we had been working to avert, instead of to hasten it. Who shall say when our boys die at eighteen, twenty, twenty-two, our girls either in their girlhood or in the first strain of their womanhood, — who shall say that they might not have passed safely through the dangers, had no vital force been unnecessarily wasted in their childhood, their infancy?

Every hour that a child sleeps is just so much investment of physical capital for years to come. Every hour after dark that a child is awake is just so much capital withdrawn. Every hour that a child lives a quiet, tranquil, joyous life of such sort as kittens live on hearths, squirrels in sunshine, is just so much investment in strength and steadiness and growth of the nervous system. Every hour that a child lives a life of excited brain-working, either in a school-room or in a ball-room, is just so much taken away from the reserved force which enables nerves to triumph through the sorrows, through the labors, through the diseases of later life. Every mouthful of wholesome food that a child eats, at seasonable hours, may be said to tell on every moment of his whole life, no matter how long it may be. Victor Hugo, the benevolent exile, has found out that to be well fed once in seven days at one meal has been enough to transform the apparent health of all the poor children in Guernsey. Who shall say that to take once in seven days, or even once in thirty days, an unwholesome supper of chicken salad and champagne may not leave as lasting effects on the constitution of a child?

If Nature would only "execute" her "sentences against evil works" more "speedily," evil works would not so thrive. The law of continuity is the hardest one for average men and women to comprehend, — or, at any rate, to obey. Seed-time and harvest in gardens and fields they have learned to understand and profit by. When we learn, also, that in the precious lives of these little ones we cannot reap what we do not sow, and we must reap all which we do sow, and that the emptiness or the richness of the harvest is not so much for us as for them, one of the first among the many things which we shall reform will be "children's parties."

AFTER-SUPPER TALK.

"AFTER-DINNER talk" has been thought of great importance. The expression has passed into literature, with many records of the good sayings it included. Kings and ministers condescend to make efforts at it; poets and philosophers — greater than kings and ministers — do not disdain to attempt to shine in it.

But nobody has yet shown what "after-supper talk" ought to be. We are not speaking now of the formal entertainment known as "a supper;" we mean the every-day evening meal in the every-day home, — the meal known heartily and commonly as "supper," among people who are neither so fashionable nor so foolish as to take still a fourth meal at hours when they ought to be asleep in bed.

This ought to be the sweetest and most precious hour of the day. It is too often neglected and lost in families. It ought to be the mother's hour; the mother's opportunity to undo any mischief the day may have done, to forestall any mischief the morrow may threaten. There is an instinctive disposition in most families to linger about the supper-table, quite unlike the eager haste which is seen at breakfast and at dinner. Work is over for the day; everybody is tired, even the little ones who have done nothing but play. The father is ready for slippers and a comfortable chair; the children are ready and eager to recount the incidents of the day. This is the time when all should be cheered, rested, and also stimulated by just the right sort of conversation, just the right sort of amusement.

The wife and mother must supply this need, must create this atmosphere. We do not mean that the father does not share the responsibility of this, as of every other hour. But this particular duty is one requiring qualities which are more essentially feminine than masculine. It wants a light touch and an *undertone* to bring out the full harmony of the ideal home evening. It must not be a bore. It must not be empty; it must not be too much like preaching; it must not be wholly like play; more than all things, it must not be always — no, not if it could be helped, not even twice — the same!. It must be that most indefinable, most recognizable thing, "a good time." Bless the children for inventing the phrase! It has, like all their phrases, an unconscious touch of sacred inspiration in it, in the selection of the good word "good," which lays peculiar benediction on all things to which it is set.

If there were no other reason against children's having lessons assigned them to study at home, we should consider this a sufficient one, that it robs them of the after-supper hour with their parents. Even if their brains could bear without injury the sixth, seventh, or eighth hour, as it may be, of study, their hearts cannot bear the being starved.

In the average family, this is the one only hour of the day when father, mother, and children can be together, free of cares and unhurried. Even to the poorest laborer's family comes now something like peace and rest forerunning the intermission of the night.

Everybody who has any artistic sense recognizes this instinctively when they see through the open doors of humble houses the father and mother and children gathered around their simple supper. Its mention has already passed into triteness in verse, so inevitably have poets felt the sacred charm of the hour.

Perhaps there is something deeper than on first thoughts would appear in the instant sense of pleasure one has in this sight; also, in the universal feeling that the evening gathering of the family is the most sacred one. Perhaps there is unconscious recognition that dangers are near at hand when night falls, and that in this hour lies, or should lie, the spell to drive them all away.

There is something almost terrible in the mingling of danger and protection, of harm and help, of good and bad, in that one thing, darkness. God "giveth his beloved sleep" in it; and in it the devil sets his worst lures, by help of it gaining many a soul which he could never get possession of in sunlight.

Mothers, fathers! cultivate "after-supper talk;" play

"after-supper games;" keep "after-supper books;" take all the good newspapers and magazines you can afford, and read them aloud "after supper." Let boys and girls bring their friends home with them at twilight, sure of a pleasant and hospitable welcome and of a good time "after supper," and parents may laugh to scorn all the temptations which town or village can set before them to draw them away from home for their evenings.

These are but hasty hints, bare suggestions. But if they rouse one heart to a new realization of what evenings at home *ought* to be, and what evenings at home too often are, they have not been spoken in vain nor out of season.

HYSTERIA IN LITERATURE.

PHYSICIANS tell us that there is no known disease, no known symptom of disease, which hysteria cannot and does not counterfeit. Most skilful surgeons are misled by its cunning into believing and pronouncing able-bodied young women to be victims of spinal disease, "stricture of the œsophagus," "gastrodynia," "paraplegia," "hemiplegia," and hundreds of other affections, with longer or shorter names. Families are thrown into disorder and distress; friends suffer untold pains of anxiety and sympathy; doctors are summoned from far and near; and all this while the vertebra, or the membrane, or the muscle, as it may be, which is so honestly believed to be diseased, and which shows every symptom of diseased action or inaction, is sound and strong, and as well able as ever it was to perform its function.

The common symptoms of hysteria everybody is familiar with, — the crying and laughing in inappropriate places, the fancied impossibility of breathing, and so forth, — which make such trouble and mortification for the embarrassed companions of hysterical persons; and which, moreover, can be very easily suppressed by a little wholesome severity, accompanied by judicious threats or sudden use of cold water. But few people know or suspect the number of diseases and conditions, supposed to be real, serious, often incurable, which are simply and solely, or in a great part, undetected hysteria. This very ignorance on the part of friends and relatives makes it almost impossible for surgeons and physicians to treat such cases properly. The probabilities are, in nine cases out of ten, that the indignant family will dismiss, as ignorant or hard-hearted, any practitioner who tells them the unvarnished truth, and proposes to treat the sufferer in accordance with it.

In the field of literature we find a hysteria as widespread, as undetected, as unmanageable as the hysteria which skulks and conquers in the field of disease.

Its commoner outbreaks everybody knows by sight and sound, and everybody except the miserably ignorant and silly despises. Yet there are to be found circles which thrill and weep in sympathetic unison with the ridiculous joys and sorrows, grotesque sentiments, and preposterous adventures of the heroes and heroines of the "Dime Novels" and novelettes, and the "Flags" and "Blades" and "Gazettes" among the lowest newspapers. But in well-regulated and intelligent households, this sort of writing is not tolerated, any more than the correlative sort of physical phenomenon would be, — the gasping, shrieking, sobbing, giggling kind of behavior in a man or woman.

But there is another and more dangerous working of

the same thing; deep, unsuspected, clothing itself with symptoms of the most defiant genuineness, it lurks and does its business in every known field of composition. Men and women are alike prone to it, though its shape is somewhat affected by sex.

Among men it breaks out often, perhaps oftenest, in violent illusions on the subject of love. They assert, declare, shout, sing, scream that they love, have loved, are loved, do and for ever will love, after methods and in manners which no decent love ever thought of mentioning. And yet, so does their weak violence ape the bearing of strength, so much does their cheat look like truth, that scores, nay, shoals of human beings go about repeating and echoing their noise, and saying, gratefully, "Yes, this is love; this is, indeed, what all true lovers must know."

These are they who proclaim names of beloved on house-tops; who strip off veils from sacred secrets and secret sacrednesses, and set them up naked for the multitude to weigh and compare. What punishment is for such beloved, Love himself only knows. It must be in store for them somewhere. Dimly one can suspect what it might be; but it will be like all Love's true secrets, — secret for ever.

These men of hysteria also take up specialties of art or science; and in their behoof rant, and exaggerate, and fabricate, and twist, and lie in such stentorian voices that reasonable people are deafened and bewildered.

They also tell common tales in such enormous

phrases, with such gigantic structure of rhetorical flourish, that the mere disproportion amounts to falsehood; and, the diseased appetite in listeners growing more and more diseased, feeding on such diseased food, it is impossible to predict what it will not be necessary for story-mongers to invent at the end of a century or so more of this.

But the worst manifestations of this disease are found in so-called religious writing. Theology, biography, especially autobiography, didactic essays, tales with a moral, — under every one of these titles it lifts up its hateful head. It takes so successfully the guise of genuine religious emotion, religious experience, religious zeal, that good people on all hands weep grateful tears as they read its morbid and unwholesome utterances. Of these are many of the long and short stories setting forth in melodramatic pictures exceptionally good or exceptionally bad children; or exceptionally pathetic and romantic careers of sweet and refined Magdalens; minute and prolonged dissections of the processes of spiritual growth; equally minute and authoritative formulas for spiritual exercises of all sorts, — "manuals of drill," so to speak, or "field tactics" for souls. Of these sorts of books, the good and the bad are almost indistinguishable from each other, except by the carefulest attention and the finest insight; overwrought, unnatural atmosphere and meaningless, shallow routine so nearly counterfeit the sound and shape of warm, true enthusiasm and wise precepts.

Where may be the remedy for this widespread and widely spreading disease among writers we do not know. It is not easy to keep up courageous faith that there is any remedy. Still Nature abhors noise and haste, and shams of all sorts. Quiet and patience are the great secrets of her force, whether it be a mountain or a soul that she would fashion. We must believe that sooner or later there will come a time in which silence shall have its dues, moderation be crowned king of speech, and melodramatic, spectacular, hysterical language be considered as disreputable as it is silly. But the most discouraging feature of the disease is its extreme contagiousness. All physicians know what a disastrous effect one hysterical patient will produce upon a whole ward in a hospital. We remember hearing a young physician once give a most amusing account of a woman who was taken to Bellevue Hospital for a hysterical cough. Her lungs, bronchia, throat, were all in perfect condition; but she coughed almost incessantly, especially on the approach of the hour for the doctor's visit to the ward. In less than one week half the women in the ward had similar coughs. A single — though it must be confessed rather terrific — application of cold water to the original offender worked a simultaneous cure upon her and all of her imitators.

Not long ago a very parallel thing was to be observed in the field of story-writing. A clever, though morbid and melodramatic writer published a novel, whose heroine, having once been an inmate of a house of ill-fame, escaped, and, finding shelter and Christian training in the home of a benevolent woman, became a model of womanly delicacy, and led a life of exquisite and artistic refinement. As to the animus and intent of this story there could be no doubt; both were good, but in atmosphere and execution it was essentially unreal, overwrought, and melodramatic. For three or four months after its publication there was a perfect outburst and overflow in newspapers and magazines of the lower order of stories, all more or less bad, some simply outrageous, and all treating, or rather pretending to treat, the same problem which had furnished theme for that novel.

Probably a close observation and collecting of the dreary statistics would bring to light a curious proof of the extent and certainty of this sort of contagion.

Reflecting on it, having it thrust in one's face at every book-counter, railway-stand, Sunday-school library, and parlor centre-table, it is hard not to wish for some supernatural authority to come sweeping through the wards, and prescribe sharp cold-water treatment all around to half drown all such writers and quite drown all their books!

JOG TROT.

THERE is etymological uncertainty about the phrase. But there is no doubt about its meaning; no doubt that it represents a good, comfortable gait, at which nobody goes nowadays.

A hundred years ago it was the fashion: in the days when railroads were not, nor telegraphs; when citizens journeyed in stages, putting up prayers in church if their journey were to be so long as from Massachusetts into Connecticut; when evil news travelled slowly by letter, and good news was carried about by men on horses; when maidens spun and wove for long, quiet, silent years at their wedding *trousseaux*, and mothers spun and wove all which sons and husbands wore; when newspapers were small and infrequent, dingy-typed and wholesomely stupid, so that no man could or would learn from them more about other men's opinions, affairs, or occupations than it concerned his practical convenience to know; when even wars were waged at slow pace,—armies sailing great distances by chance winds, or plodding on foot for thousands of miles, and fighting doggedly hand to hand at sight; when fortunes also were slowly made by simple, honest growths,—no men excepting freebooters and pirates becoming rich in a day.

It would seem treason or idiocy to sigh for these old days,—treason to ideas of progress, stupid idiocy unaware that it is well off. Is not to-day brilliant, marvellous, beautiful? Has not living become subject to a magician's "presto"? Are we not decked in the whole of color, feasted on all that shape and sound and flavor can give? Are we not wiser each moment than we were the moment before? Do not the blind see, the deaf hear, and the crippled dance? Has not Nature surrendered to us? Art and science, are they not our slaves,—coining money and running mills? Have we not built and multiplied religions, till each man, even the most irreligious, can have his own? Is not what is called the "movement of the age" going on at the highest rate of speed and of sound? Shall we complain that we are maddened by the racket, out of breath with the spinning and whirling, and dying of the strain of it all? What is a man, more or less? What are one hundred and twenty millions of men, more or less? What is quiet in comparison with riches? or digestion and long life in comparison with knowledge? When we are added up in the universal reckoning of races, there will be small mention of individuals. Let us be disinterested. Let us sacrifice ourselves, and, above all, our children, to raise the general average of human invention and attainment to the highest possible mark. To be sure, we are working in the dark. We do not know, not even if we are Huxley do we know, at what point in the grand, universal scale we shall ultimately come in. We know, or think we know, about how far below us stand the gorilla and the seal. We patronize them kindly for learning to turn hand-organs or eat from porringers. Let us hope that, if we have brethren of higher races on other planets, they will be as generously appreciative of our little all when we have done it; but, meanwhile, let us never be deterred from our utmost endeavor by any base and envious misgivings that possibly we may not be the last and highest work of the Creator, and in a fair way to reach very soon the final climax of all which created intelligences can be or become. Let us make the best of dyspepsia, paralysis, insanity, and the death of our children. Perhaps we can do as much in forty years, working night and day, as we could in seventy, working only by day; and the five out of twelve children that live to grow up can perpetuate the names and the methods of their fathers. It is a comfort to believe, as we are told, that the world can never lose an iota that it has gained; that progress is the great law of the universe. It is consoling to verify this truth by looking backward, and seeing how each age has made use of the wrecks of the preceding one as material for new structures on different plans. What are we that we should mention our preference for being put to some other use, more immediately remunerative to ourselves!

We must be all wrong if we are not in sympathy with the age in which we live. We might as well be dead as not keep up with it. But which of us does not sometimes wish in his heart of hearts, that he had been born long enough ago to have been boon companion of his great-grandfather, and have gone respectably and in due season to his grave at a good jog trot?

THE JOYLESS AMERICAN.

IT is easy to fancy that a European, on first reaching these shores, might suppose that he had chanced to arrive upon a day when some great public calamity had saddened the heart of the nation. It would be quite safe to assume that out of the first five hundred faces which he sees there will not be ten wearing a smile, and not fifty, all told, looking as if they ever could smile. If this statement sounds extravagant to any man, let him try the experiment, for one week, of noting down, in his walks about town, every face he sees which has a radiantly cheerful expression. The chances are that at the end of his seven days he will not have entered seven faces in his note-book without being aware at the moment of some conscientious difficulty in permitting himself to call them positively and unmistakably cheerful.

The truth is, this wretched and joyless expression on the American face is so common that we are hardened to seeing it, and look for nothing better. Only when by chance some blessed, rollicking, sunshiny boy or girl or man or woman flashes the beam of a laughing countenance into the level gloom do we even know that we are in the dark. Witness the instant effect of the entrance of such a person into an omnibus or a car. Who has not observed it? Even the most stolid and apathetic soul relaxes a little. The unconscious intruder, simply by smiling, has set the blood moving more quickly in the veins of every human being who sees him. He is, for the moment, the personal benefactor of every one; if he had handed about money or bread, it would have been a philanthropy of less value.

What is to be done to prevent this acrid look of misery from becoming an organic characteristic of our people? "Make them play more," says one philosophy. No doubt they need to "play more;" but, when one looks at the average expression of a Fourth of July crowd, one doubts if ever so much multiplication of that kind of holiday would mend the matter. No doubt we work for too many days in the year, and play for too few; but, after all, it is the heart and the spirit and the expression that we bring to our work, and not those that we bring to our play, by which our real vitality must be tested and by which our faces will be stamped. If we do not work healthfully, reasoningly, moderately, thankfully, joyously, we shall have neither moderation nor gratitude nor joy in our play. And here is the hopelessness, here is the root of the trouble, of the joyless American face. The worst of all demons, the demon of unrest and overwork, broods in the very sky of this land. Blue and clear and crisp and sparkling as our atmosphere is, it cannot or does not exorcise the spell. Any old man can count on the fingers of one hand the persons he has known who led lives of serene, unhurried content, made for themselves occupations and not tasks, and died at last what might be called natural deaths.

"What, then?" says the congressional candidate from Mettibemps; the "new contributor" to the oceanic magazine; Mrs. Potiphar, from behind her liveries; and poor Dives, senior, from Wall Street; "Are we to give up all ambition?" God forbid. But, because one has a goal, must one be torn by poisoned spurs? We see on the Corso, in the days of the Carnival, what speed can be made by horses under torture. Shall we try those methods and that pace on our journeys?

So long as the American is resolved to do in one day the work of two, to make in one year the fortune of his whole life and his children's, to earn before he is forty the reputation which belongs to threescore and ten, so long he will go about the streets wearing his present abject, pitiable, overwrought, joyless look. But, even without a change of heart or a reform of habits, he might better his countenance a little, if he would. Even if he does not feel like smiling, he might smile, if he tried; and that would be something. The muscles are all there; they count the same in the American as in the French or the Irish face; they relax easily in youth; the trick can be learned. And even a trick of it is better than none of it. Laughing masters might be as well paid as dancing masters to help on society! "Smiling made Easy" or the "Complete Art of Looking Good-natured" would be as taking titles on booksellers' shelves as "The Complete Letter-writer" or "Handbook of Behavior." And nobody can calculate what might be the moral and spiritual results if it could only become the fashion to pursue this branch of the fine arts. Surliness of heart must melt a little under the simple effort to smile. A man will inevitably be a little less of a bear for trying to wear the face of a Christian.

"He who laughs can commit no deadly sin," said the wise and sweet-hearted woman who was mother of Goethe.

SPIRITUAL TEETHING

MILK for babes; but, when they come to the age for meat of doctrine, teeth must be cut. It is harder work for souls than for bodies; but the processes are wonderfully parallel, — the results too, alas! If clergymen knew the symptoms of spiritual disease and death, as well as doctors do of disease and death of the flesh, and if the lists were published at end of each year and month and week, what a record would be shown! "Mortality in Brooklyn, or New York, or Philadelphia for the week ending July 7th." We are so used to the curt heading of the little paragraph that our eye glances idly away from it, and we do not realize its sadness. By tens and by scores they have gone, — the men, the women, the babies; in hundreds new mourners are going about the streets, week by week. We are as familiar with black as with scarlet, with the hearse as with the pleasure-carriage; and yet "so dies in human hearts the thought of death" that we can be merry.

But, if we knew as well the record of sick and dying and dead souls, our hearts would break. The air would be dark and stifling. We should be afraid to move, lest we might hasten the last hour of some neighbor's spiritual breath. Ah, how often have we unconsciously spoken the one word which was poison to his fever!

Of the spiritual deaths, as of the physical, more than half take place in the period of teething. The more one thinks of the parallelism, the closer it looks, until the likeness seems as droll as dismal. Oh, the sweet, unquestioning infancy which takes its food from the nearest breast; which knows but three things, — hunger and food and sleep! There is only a little space for this delight. In our seventh month we begin to be wretched. We drink our milk, but we are aware of a constant desire to bite; doubts which we do not know by name, needs for which there is no ready supply, make us restless. Now comes the old-school doctor, and thrusts in his lancet too soon. We suffer, we bleed; we are supposed to be relieved. The tooth is said to be "through."

Through! Oh, yes; through before its time. Through to no purpose. In a week, or a year, the wounded flesh, or soul, has reasserted its right, shut down on the tooth, making a harder surface than ever, a cicatrized crust, out of which it will take double time and double strength for the tooth to break.

The gentle doctor gives us a rubber ring, it has a bad taste; or an ivory one, it is too hard and hurts us. But we gnaw and gnaw, and fancy the new pain a little easier to bear than the old. Probably it is; probably the tooth gets through a little quicker for the days and nights of gnawing. But what a picture of patient misery is a baby with its rubber ring! Really one sees sometimes in the little puckered, twisting face such grotesque prophecy of future conflicts, such likeness to the soul's processes of grappling with problems, that it is uncanny.

When we come to the analysis of the diseases incident to the teething period, and the treatment of them, the similitude is as close.

We have sharp, sudden inflammations; we have subtle and more deadly things, which men do not detect till it is, in nine cases out of ten, too late to cure them, — like water on the brain; and we have slow wastings away; atrophies, which are worse than death, leaving life enough to prolong death indefinitely, being as it were living deaths.

Who does not know poor souls in all stages of all these, — outbreaks of rebellion against all forms, all creeds, all proprieties; secret adoptions of perilous delusions, fatal errors; and slow settling down into indifferentism or narrow dogmatism, the two worst living deaths?

These are they who live. Shall we say any thing of those of us who die between our seventh and eighteenth spiritual month? They never put on babies' tombstones "Died of teething." There is always a special name for the special symptom or set of symptoms which characterized the last days. But the mother believes and the doctor knows that, if it had not been for the teeth that were coming just at that time, the fever or the croup would not have killed the child.

Now we come to the treatments; and here again the parallelism is so close as to be ludicrous. The lancet and the rubber ring fail. We are still restless, and scream and cry. Then our self-sacrificing nurses walk with us; they rock us, they swing us, they toss us up and down, they jounce us from top to bottom, till the wonder is that every organ in our bodies is not displaced. They beat on glass and tin and iron to distract our attention and drown out our noise by a bigger one; they shake back and forth before our eyes all things that glitter and blaze; they shout and sing songs; the house and the neighborhood are searched and racked for something which will "amuse" the baby. Then, when we will no longer be "amused," and when all this restlessness outside and around us, added to the restlessness inside us, has driven us more than frantic, and the day or the night of their well-meant clamor is nearly over, their strength worn out, and their wits at end, — then comes the "soothing syrup," deadliest weapon of all. This we cannot resist. If there be they who are mighty enough to pour it down our throats, physically or spiritually, to sleep we must go, and asleep we must stay so long as the effect of the dose lasts.

It is of this we oftenest die, — not in a day or a year, but after many days and many years; when in some sharp crisis we need for our salvation the force which should have been developing in our infancy, the muscle or the nerve which should have been steadily growing strong till that moment. But the force is not there; the muscle is weak; the nerve paralyzed; and we die at twenty of a light fever, we fall down at twenty, under sudden grief or temptation, because of our long sleeps under soothing syrups when we were babies.

Oh, good nurses and doctors of souls, let them cut their own teeth, in the natural ways. Let them scream if they must, but keep you still on one side; give them no false helps; let them alone so far as it is possible for love and sympathy to do so. Man is the only animal that has trouble from the growing of the teeth in his body. It must be his own fault somehow that he has that; and he has evidently been always conscious of a likeness between this difficulty and perversion of a process natural to his body, and the difficulty and perversion of his getting sensible and just opinions; for it has passed into the immortality of a proverb that a shrewd man is a man who has "cut his eye-teeth;" and the four last teeth, which we get late in life, and which cost many people days of real illness, are called in all tongues, all countries, "wisdom teeth!"

GLASS HOUSES.

WHO would live in one, if he could help it? And who wants to throw stones?

But who lives in any thing else, nowadays? And how much better off are they who never threw a stone in their lives than the rude mob who throw them all the time?

Really, the proverb might as well be blotted out from our books and dropped from our speech. It has no longer use or meaning.

It is becoming a serious question what shall be done, or rather what can be done, to secure to fastidious people some show and shadow of privacy in their homes. The silly and vulgar passion of people for knowing all about their neighbors' affairs, which is bad enough while it takes shape merely in idle gossip of mouth, is something terrible when it is exalted into a regular market demand of the community, and fed by a regular market supply from all who wish to print what the community will read.

We do not know which is worse in this traffic, the buyer or the seller; we think, on the whole, the buyer.

But then he is again a seller; and so there it is,—wheel within wheel, cog upon cog. And, since all these sellers must earn their bread and butter, the more one searches for a fair point of attacking the evil, the more he is perplexed.

The man who writes must, if he needs pay for his work, write what the man who prints will buy. The man who prints must print what the people who read will buy. Upon whom, then, shall we lay earnest hands? Clearly, upon the last buyer,—upon him who reads. But things have come to such a pass already that to point out to the average American that it is vulgar and also unwholesome to devour with greedy delight all sorts of details about his neighbors' business seems as hopeless and useless as to point out to the currie-eater or the whiskey-drinker the bad effects of fire and strychnine upon mucous membranes. The diseased palate craves what has made it diseased,—craves it more, and more, and more. In case of stomachs, Nature has a few simple inventions of her own for bringing reckless abuses to a stand-still,—dyspepsia, and delirium-tremens, and so on.

But she takes no account, apparently, of the diseased conditions of brains incident to the long use of unwholesome or poisonous intellectual food. Perhaps she never anticipated this class of excesses. And, if there were to be a precisely correlative punishment, it is to be feared it would fall more heavily on the least guilty offender. It is not hard to fancy a poor soul who, having been condemned to do reporters' duty for some years, and having been forced to dwell and dilate upon scenes and details which his very soul revolted from mentioning, — it is not hard to fancy such a soul visited at last by a species of delirium-tremens, in which the speeches of men who had spoken, the gowns of women who had danced, the faces, the figures, the furniture of celebrities, should all be mixed up in a grotesque phantasmagoria of torture, before which he should writhe as helplessly and agonizingly as the poor whiskey-drinker before his snakes. But it would be a cruel misplacement of punishment. All the while the true guilty would be placidly sitting down at still further unsavory banquets, which equally helpless providers were driven to furnish!

The evil is all the harder to deal with, also, because it is like so many evils, — all, perhaps, — only a diseased outgrowth, from a legitimate and justifiable thing. It is our duty to sympathize; it is our privilege and pleasure to admire. No man lives to himself alone; no man can; no man ought. It is right that we should know about our neighbors all which will help us to help them, to be just to them, to avoid them, if need be; in short, all which we need to know for their or our reasonable and fair advantage. It is right, also, that we should know about men who are or have been great all which can enable us to understand their greatness; to profit, to imitate, to revere; all that will help us to remember whatever is worth remembering. There is education in this; it is experience, it is history.

But how much of what is written, printed, and read to-day about the men and women of to-day comes under these heads? It is unnecessary to do more than ask the question. It is still more unnecessary to do more than ask how many of the men and women of to-day, whose names have become almost as stereotyped a part of public journals as the very titles of the journals themselves, have any claim to such prominence. But all these considerations seem insignificant by side of the intrinsic one of the vulgarity of the thing, and its impudent ignoring of the most sacred rights of individuals. That there are here and there weak fools who like to see their names and most trivial movements chronicled in newspapers cannot be denied. But they are few. And their silly pleasure is very small in the aggregate compared with the annoyance and pain suffered by sensitive and refined people from these merciless invasions of their privacy. No precautions can forestall them, no reticence prevent; nothing, apparently, short of dying outright, can set one free. And even then it is merely leaving the torture behind, a harrowing legacy to one's friends; for tombs are even less sacred than houses. Memory, friendship, obligation,—all are lost sight of in the greed of desire to make an effective sketch, a surprising revelation, a neat analysis, or perhaps an adroit implication of honor to one's self by reason of an old association with greatness. Private letters and private conversations, which may touch living hearts in a thousand sore spots, are hawked about as coolly as if they had been old clothes, left too long unredeemed in the hands of the pawn-broker! "Dead men tell no tales," says the proverb. One wishes they could! We should miss some spicy contributions to magazine and newspaper literature; and a sudden silence would fall upon some loud-mouthed living.

But we despair of any cure for this evil. No ridicule, no indignation seems to touch it. People must make the best they can of their glass houses; and, if the stones come too fast, take refuge in the cellars.

THE OLD-CLOTHES MONGER IN JOURNALISM.

THE old-clothes business has never been considered respectable. It is supposed to begin and to end with cheating; it deals with very dirty things. It would be hard to mention a calling of lower repute. From the men who come to your door with trays of abominable china vases on their heads, and are ready to take any sort of rags in payment for them, down — or up? — to the bigger wretches who advertise that "ladies and gentlemen can obtain the highest price for their cast-off clothing by calling at No. so and so, on such a street," they are all alike odious and despicable.

We wonder when we find anybody who is not an abject Jew, engaged in the business. We think we can recognize the stamp of the disgusting traffic on their very faces. It is by no means uncommon to hear it said of a sorry sneak, "He looks like an old-clothes dealer."

But what shall we say of the old-clothes mongers in journalism? By the very name we have defined, described them, and pointed them out. If only we could make the name such a badge of disgrace that every member of the fraternity should forthwith betake him or herself to some sort of honest labor!

These are they who crowd the columns of our daily newspapers with the dreary, monotonous, worthless, scandalous tales of what other men and women did, are doing, or will do, said, say, or will say, wore, wear, or will wear, thought, think, or will think, ate, eat, or will eat, drank, drink, or will drink: and if there be any other verb coming under the head of "to do, to be, to suffer," add that to the list, and the old-clothes monger will furnish you with something to fill out the phrase.

These are they who patch out their miserable, little, sham "properties" for mock representations of life, by scraps from private letters, bits of conversation overheard on piazzas, in parlors, in bedrooms, by odds and ends of untrustworthy statements picked up at railway-stations, church-doors, and offices of all sorts, by impudent inferences and suppositions, and guesses about other people's affairs, by garblings and partial quotings, and, if need be, by wholesale lyings.

The trade is on the increase,—rapidly, fearfully on the increase. Every large city, every summer watering-place, is more or less infested with this class of dealers. The goods they have to furnish are more and more in demand. There is hardly a journal in the country but has column after column full of their tattered wares; there is hardly a man or woman in the country but buys them.

There is, perhaps, no remedy. Human nature has

not yet shed all the monkey. A lingering and grovelling baseness in the average heart delights in this sort of cast-off clothes of fellow-worms. But if the trade must continue, can we not insist that the profits be shared? If A is to receive ten dollars for quoting B's remarks at a private dinner yesterday, shall not B have a small percentage on the sale? Clearly, this is only justice. And in cases where the wares are simply stolen, shall there be no redress? Here is an opening for a new Bureau. How well its advertisements would read: —

"Ladies and gentlemen wishing to dispose of their old opinions, sentiments, feelings, and so forth, and also of the more interesting facts in their personal history, can obtain good prices for the same at No. — Tittle-tattle street. Inquire at the door marked 'Regular and Special Correspondence.'

"N. B. — Persons willing to be reported *verbatim* will receive especial consideration."

We commend this brief suggestion of a new business to all who are anxious to make a living and not particular how they make it. Perhaps the class of whom we have been speaking would find it profitable to set it up as a branch of their own calling. It is quite possible that nobody else in the country would like to meddle with it.

THE COUNTRY LANDLORD'S SIDE.

IT is only one side, to be sure. But it is the side of which we hear least. The quarrel is like all quarrels, — it takes two to make it; but as, of those two, one is only one, and the other is from ten to a hundred, it is easy to see which side will do most talking in setting forth its grievances.

"It is naught, it is naught, saith the buyer; and when he is gone his way then he boasteth." We are oftener reminded of this text of Scripture than of any other when we listen to conversations in regard to boarders in country houses.

"Oh, let me tell you of such a nice place we have found to board in the country. It is only — miles from Mt. —— or Lake ——; the drives are delightful, and board is only $7 a week."

"Is the table a good one?"

"Oh, yes; very good for the country. We had good butter and milk, and eggs in abundance. Meats, of course, are never very good in the country. But everybody gained a pound a week; and we are going again this year, if they have not raised their prices."

Then this model of a city woman, in search of country lodgings, sits down and writes to the landlord:—

"Dear Sir, — We would like to secure our old rooms in your house for the whole of July and August. As we shall remain so long a time, we hope you may be willing to count all the children at half-price. Last year, you may remember, we paid full price for the two eldest, the twins, who are not yet quite fourteen. I hope, also, that Mrs. ——— has better arrangements for washing this summer, and will allow us to have our own servant to do the washing for the whole family. If these terms suit you, the price for my family — eight children, myself, and servant — would be $38.50 a week. Perhaps, if the servant takes the entire charge of my rooms, you would call it $37; as, of course, that would save the time of your own servants."

Then the country landlord hesitates. He is not positively sure of filling all his rooms for the season. Thirty-seven dollars a week would be, he thinks, better than nothing. In his simplicity, he supposes that, if he confers, as he certainly does, a favor on Mrs. ——, by receiving her great family on such low terms, she will be thoroughly well disposed toward him and his house, and will certainly not be over-exacting in matter of accommodations. In an evil hour, he consents; they come, and he begins to reap his reward. The twins are stout boys, as large as men, and much hungrier. The baby is a sickly child of eighteen months, and requires especial diet, which must be prepared at especial and inconvenient hours, in the crowded little kitchen. The other five children are average boys and girls, between the ages of three and twelve, eat certainly as much as five grown people, and make twice as much trouble. The servant is a slow, inefficient, impudent Irish girl, who spends the greater part of four days in doing the family washing, and makes the other servants uncomfortable and cross.

If this were all; but this is not. Mrs. ———, who writes to all her friends boastingly of the cheap summer quarters that she has found, and who gains by the village shop-keeper's scales a pound of flesh a week, habitually finds fault with the food, with the mattresses, with the chairs, with the rag-carpets, with every thing, in short, down to the dust and the flies, for neither of which last the poor landlord could be legitimately held responsible. This is not an exaggerated picture. Everybody who has boarded in country places in the summer has known dozens of such women. Every country landlord can produce dozens of such letters, and of letters still more exacting and unreasonable.

The average city man or woman who goes to a country house to board, goes expecting what it is in the nature of things impossible that they should have. The man expects to have boots blacked and hot water ready, and a bell to ring for both. What experienced country boarder has not laughed in his sleeve to see such an one, newly arrived, putting his head out snappingly, like a turtle, from his doorway, and calling to chance passers, "How d'ye get at anybody in this house?"

If it is a woman, she expects that the tea will be of the finest flavor, and never boiled; that steaks will be porter-house steaks; that green peas will be in plenty; and that the American girl, who is chambermaid for the summer, and school-teacher in the winter, and who, ten to one, could put her to the blush in five minutes by superior knowledge on many subjects, will enter and leave her room and wait upon her at the table with the silent respectfulness of a trained city servant.

This is all very silly. But it happens. At the end of every summer hundreds of disappointed city people go back to their homes grumbling about country food and country ways. Hundreds of tired and discouraged wives of country landlords sit down in their houses, at last emptied, and vow a vow that never again will they take "city folks to board." But the great law of supply and demand is too strong for them. The city must come out of itself for a few weeks, and get oxygen for its lungs, sunlight for its eyes, and rest for its overworked brain. The country must open its arms, whether it will or not, and share its blessings. And so the summers and the summerings go on, and there are always to be heard in the land the voices of murmuring boarders, and of landlords deprecating, vindicating. We confess that our sympathies are with the landlords. The average country landlord is an honest, well-meaning man, whose idea of the profit to be made "off boarders" is so moderate and simple that the keepers of city boarding-houses would laugh it and him to scorn. If this were not so, would he be found undertaking to lodge and feed people for one dollar or a dollar and a half a day? Neither does he dream of asking them, even at this low price, to fare as he fares. The "Excelsior" mattresses, at which they cry out in disgust, are beds of down in comparison with the straw "tick" on which he and his wife sleep soundly and contentedly. He has paid $4.50 for each mattress, as a special concession to what he understands city prejudice to require. The cheap painted chamber-sets are holiday adorning by the side of the cherry and pine in the bedrooms of his family. He buys fresh meat every day for dinner; and nobody can understand the importance of this fact who is not familiar with the habit of salt-pork and codfish in our rural districts. That the meat is tough, pale, stringy is not his fault; no other is to be bought. Stetson, himself, if he dealt with this country butcher, could do no better. Vegetables? Yes, he has planted them. If we look out of our windows, we can see them on their winding way. They will be ripe by and by. He never tasted peas in his life before the Fourth of July, or cucumbers before the middle of August. He hears that there are such things; but he thinks they must be "dreadful unhealthy, them things forced out of season,"—and, whether healthy or not, he can't get them. We couldn't ourselves, if we were keeping house in the same township. To be sure, we might send to the cities for them, and be served with such as were wilted to begin with, and would arrive utterly unfit to be eaten at end of their day's journey, costing double their market price in the added express charge. We should not do any such thing. We should do just as he does, make the best of "plum sauce," or even dried apples. We should not make our sauce with molasses, probably; but he does not know that sugar is better; he honestly likes molasses best. As for saleratus in the bread, as for fried meat, and fried doughnuts, and ubiquitous pickles,—all those things have he, and his fathers before him, eaten, and, he thinks, thriven on from time immemorial. He will listen incredulously to all we say about the effects of alkalies, the change of fats to injurious oils by frying, the indigestibility of pickles, &c.; for, after all, the unanswerable fact remains on his side, though he may be too polite or too slow to make use of it in the argument, that, having fed on these poisons all his life, he can easily thrash us to-day, and his wife and daughters can and do work from morning till night, while ours must lie down and rest by noon. In spite of all this, he will do what he can to humor our whims. Never yet have we seen the country boarding-house where kindly and persistent remonstrance would not introduce the gridiron and banish the frying-pan, and obtain at least an attempt at yeast-bread. Good, patient, long-suffering country people! The only wonder to us is that they tolerate so pleasantly, make such effort to gratify, the preferences and prejudices of city men and women, who come and who remain strangers among them; and who, in so many instances, behave from first to last as if they were of a different race, and knew nothing of any common bonds of humanity and Christianity.

THE GOOD STAFF OF PLEASURE.

IN an inn in Berchtesgaden, Bavaria, where I dined every day for three weeks, one summer, I made the acquaintance of a little maid called Gretchen. She stood all day long washing dishes, in a dark passage-way which communicated in some mysterious fashion with cellar, kitchen, dining-room, and main hall of the inn. From one or other of these quarters Gretchen was sharply called so often that it was a puzzle to know how she contrived to wash so much as a cup or a plate in the course of the day. Poor child! I am afraid she did most of her work after dark; for I sometimes left her standing there at ten o'clock at night. She was blanched and shrunken from fatigue and lack of sun-light. I doubt if ever, unless perhaps on some exceptional Sunday, she knew the sensation of a full breath of pure air or a warm sunbeam on her face.

But whenever I passed her she smiled, and there was never-failing good-cheer in her voice when she said "Good-morning." Her uniform atmosphere of contentedness so impressed and surprised me that, at last, I said to Franz, the head waiter, —

"What makes Gretchen so happy? She has a hard

life, always standing in that narrow dark place, washing dishes."

Franz was phlegmatic, and spoke very little English. He shrugged his shoulders, in sign of assent that Gretchen's life was a hard one, and added, —

"Ja, ja. She likes because all must come at her door. There will be no one which will say not nothing if they go by."

That was it. Almost every hour some human voice said pleasantly to her, "Good-morning, Gretchen," or "It is a fine day;" or, if no word were spoken, there would be a friendly nod and smile. For nowhere in kind-hearted, simple Germany do human beings pass by other human beings, as we do in America, without so much as a turn of the head to show recognition of humanity in common.

This one little pleasure kept Gretchen not only alive, but comparatively glad. Her body suffered for want of sun and air. There was no helping that, by any amount of spiritual compensation, so long as she must stand, year in and year out, in a close, dark corner, and do hard drudgery. But, if she had stood in that close, dark corner, doing that hard drudgery, and had had no pleasure to comfort her, she would have been dead in three months.

If all men and women could realize the power, the might of even a small pleasure, how much happier the world would be! and how much longer bodies and souls both would bear up under living! Sensitive people realize it to the very core of their being. They know that often and often it happens to them to be revived, kindled, strengthened, to a degree which they could not describe, and which they hardly comprehend, by some little thing, — some word of praise, some token of remembrance, some proof of affection or recognition. They know, too, that strength goes out of them, just as inexplicably, just as fatally, when for a space, perhaps even a short space, all these are wanting.

People who are not sensitive also come to find this out, if they are tender. They are by no means inseparable, — tenderness and sensitiveness ; if they were, human nature would be both more comfortable and more agreeable. But tender people alone can be just to sensitive ones ; living in close relations with them, they learn what they need, and, so far as they can, supply it, even when they wonder a little, and perhaps grow a little weary.

We see a tender and just mother sometimes sighing because one over-sensitive child must be so much more gently restrained or admonished than the rest. But she has her reward for every effort to adjust her methods to the instrument she does not quite understand. If she doubts this, she has only to look on the right hand and the left, and see the effect of careless, brutal dealing with finely strung, sensitive natures.

We see, also, many men, — good, generous, kindly, but not sensitive-souled, — who have learned that the sunshine of their homes all depends on little things, which it would never have entered into their busy and composed hearts to think of doing, or saying, or providing, if they had not discovered that without them their wives droop, and with them they keep well.

People who are neither tender nor sensitive can neither comprehend nor meet these needs. Alas! that there are so many such people; or that, if there must be just so many, as I suppose there must, they are not distinguishable at first sight, by some mark of color, or shape, or sound, so that one might avoid them, or at least know what to expect in entering into relation with them. Woe be to any sensitive soul whose life must, in spite of itself, take tone and tint from daily and intimate intercourse with such! No bravery, no philosophy, no patience can save it from a slow death. But, while the subtlest and most stimulating pleasures which the soul knows come to it through its affections, and are, therefore, so to speak, at every man's mercy, there is still left a world of possibility of enjoyment, to which we can help ourselves, and which no man can hinder.

And just here it is, I think, that many persons, especially those who are hard-worked, and those who have some special trouble to bear, make great mistake. They might, perhaps, say at hasty first sight that it would be selfish to aim at providing themselves with pleasures. Not at all. Not one whit more than it is for them to buy a bottle of Ayer's Sarsaparilla (if they do not know better) to "cleanse their blood" in the spring! Probably a dollar's worth of almost any thing out of any other shop than a druggist's would "cleanse their blood" better, — a geranium, for instance, or a photograph, or a concert, or a book, or even fried oysters, — any thing, no matter what, so it is innocent, which gives them a little pleasure, breaks in on the monotony of their work or their trouble, and makes them have for one half-hour a "good time." Those who have near and dear ones to remember these things for them need no such words as I am writing here. Heaven forgive them if, being thus blessed, they do not thank God daily and take courage.

But lonely people, and people whose kin are not kind or wise in these things, must learn to minister even in such ways to themselves. It is not selfish. It is not foolish. It is wise. It is generous. Each contented look on a human face is reflected in every other human face which sees it; each growth in a human soul is a blessing to every other human soul which comes in contact with it.

Here will come in, for many people, the bitter restrictions of poverty. There are so many men and women to whom it would seem simply a taunt to advise them to spend, now and then, a dollar for a pleasure. That the poor must go cold and hungry has never seemed to me the hardest feature in their lot; there are worse deprivations than that of food or raiment, and this very thing is one of them. This is a point for charitable people to remember, even more than they do.

We appreciate this when we give some plum-pudding and turkey at Christmas, instead of all coal and flannel. But, any day in the year, a picture on the wall might perhaps be as comforting as a blanket on the bed; and, at any rate, would be good for twelve months, while the blanket would help but six. I have seen an Irish mother, in a mud hovel, turn red with delight at a rattle for her baby, when I am quite sure she would have been indifferently grateful for a pair of socks.

Food and physicians and money are and always will be on the earth. But a "merry heart" is a "continual feast," and "doeth good like a medicine;" and "loving favor" is "chosen," "rather than gold and silver."

WANTED.—A HOME.

NOTHING can be meaner than that "Misery should love company." But the proverb is founded on an original principle in human nature, which it is no use to deny and hard work to conquer. I have been uneasily conscious of this sneaking sin in my own soul, as I have read article after article in the English newspapers and magazines on the "decadence of the home spirit in English family life, as seen in the large towns and the metropolis." It seems that the English are as badly off as we. There, also, men are wide-awake and gay at clubs and races, and sleepy and morose in their own houses; "sons lead lives independent of their fathers and apart from their sisters and mothers;" "girls run about as they please, without care or guidance." This state of things is "a spreading social evil," and men are at their wit's end to know what is to be done about it. They are ransacking "national character and customs, religion, and the particular tendency of the present literary and scientific thought, and the teaching and preaching of the public press," to find out the root of the trouble. One writer ascribes it to the "exceeding restlessness and the desire to be doing something which are predominant and indomitable in the Anglo-Saxon race;" another to the passion which almost all families have for seeming richer and more fashionable than their means will allow. In these, and in most of their other theories, they are only working round and round, as doctors so often do, in the dreary circle of symptomatic results, without so much as touching or perhaps suspecting their real centre. How many people are blistered for spinal disease, or blanketed for rheumatism, when the real trouble is a little fiery spot of inflammation in the lining of the stomach! and all these difficulties in the outworks are merely the creaking of the machinery, because the central engine does not work properly. Blisters and blankets may go on for seventy years coddling the poor victim; but he will stay ill to the last if his stomach be not set right.

There is a close likeness between the doctor's high-sounding list of remote symptoms, which he is treating as primary diseases, and the hue and outcry about the decadence of the home spirit, the prevalence of excessive and improper amusements, club-houses, billiard-rooms, theatres, and so forth, which are "the banes of homes."

The trouble is in the homes. Homes are stupid, homes are dreary, homes are insufferable. If one can be pardoned for the Irishism of such a saying, homes are their own worst "banes." If homes were what they should be, nothing under heaven could be invented which could be bane to them, which would do more than serve as useful foil to set off their better cheer, their pleasanter ways, their wholesomer joys.

Whose fault is it that they are not so? Fault is a heavy word. It includes generations in its pitiless entail. Sufficient for the day is the evil thereof is but one side of the truth. No day is sufficient unto the evil thereof is the other. Each day has to bear burdens passed down from so many other days; each person has to bear burdens so complicated, so interwoven with the burdens of others; each person's fault is so fevered and swollen by faults of others, that there is no disentangling the question of responsibility, Every thing is everybody's fault is the simplest and fairest way of putting it. It is everybody's fault that the average home is stupid, dreary, insufferable, — a place from which fathers fly to clubs, boys and girls to streets. But when we ask who can do most to remedy this, — in whose hands it most lies to fight the fight against the tendencies to monotony, stupidity, and instability which are inherent in human nature, — then the answer is clear and loud. It is the work of women; this is the true mission of women, their "right" divine and unquestionable, and including most emphatically the "right to labor."

To create and sustain the atmosphere of a home, — it is easily said in a very few words; but how many women have done it? How many women can say to themselves or others that this is their aim? To keep house well women often say they desire. But keeping house well is another affair, — I had almost said it has nothing to do with creating a home. That is not true, of course; comfortable living, as regards food and fire and clothes, can do much to help on a home. Nevertheless, with one exception, the best homes I have ever seen were in houses which were not especially well kept; and the very worst I have ever known were presided (I mean tyrannized) over by "perfect housekeepers."

All creators are single-aimed. Never will the painter, sculptor, writer lose sight of his art. Even in the intervals of rest and diversion which are necessary to his health and growth, every thing he sees ministers to his passion. Consciously or unconsciously, he makes each shape, color, incident his own; sooner or later it will enter into his work.

So it must be with the woman who will create a home. There is an evil fashion of speech which says it is a narrowing and narrow life that a woman leads who cares only, works only for her husband and children; that a higher, more imperative thing is that she herself be developed to her utmost. Even so clear and strong a writer as Frances Cobbe, in her otherwise admirable essay on the "Final Cause of Woman," falls into this shallowness of words, and speaks of women who live solely for their families as "adjectives."

In the family relation so many women are nothing more, so many women become even less, that human conception may perhaps be forgiven for losing sight of the truth, the ideal. Yet in women it is hard to forgive it. Thinking clearly, she should see that a creator can never be an adjective; and that a woman who creates and sustains a home, and under whose hands children grow up to be strong and pure men and women, is a creator, second only to God.

Before she can do this, she must have development; in and by the doing of this comes constant development; the higher her development, the more perfect her work; the instant her own development is arrested, her creative power stops. All science, all art, all religion, all experience of life, all knowledge of men—will help her; the stars in their courses can be won to fight for her. Could she attain the utmost of knowledge, could she have all possible human genius, it would be none too much. Reverence holds its breath and goes softly, perceiving what it is in this woman's power to do; with what divine patience, steadfastness, and inspiration she must work.

Into the home she will create, monotony, stupidity, antagonisms cannot come. Her foresight will provide occupations and amusements; her loving and alert diplomacy will fend off disputes. Unconsciously, every member of her family will be as clay in her hands. More anxiously than any statesman will she meditate on the wisdom of each measure, the bearing of each word. The least possible governing which is compatible with order will be her first principle; her second, the greatest possible influence which is compatible with the growth of individuality. Will the woman whose brain and heart are working these problems, as applied to a household, be an adjective? be idle?

She will be no more an adjective than the sun is an

adjective in the solar system; no more idle than Nature is idle. She will be perplexed; she will be weary; she will be disheartened, sometimes. All creators, save One, have known these pains and grown strong by them. But she will never withdraw her hand for one instant. Delays and failures will only set her to casting about for new instrumentalities. She will press all things into her service. She will master sciences, that her boys' evenings need not be dull. She will be worldly wise, and render to Cæsar his dues, that her husband and daughters may have her by their side in all their pleasures. She will invent, she will surprise, she will forestall, she will remember, she will laugh, she will listen, she will be young, she will be old, and she will be three times loving, loving, loving.

This is too hard? There is the house to be kept? And there are poverty and sickness, and there is not time?

Yes, it is hard. And there is the house to be kept; and there are poverty and sickness; but, God be praised, there is time. A minute is time. In one minute may live the essence of all. I have seen a beggar-woman make half an hour of home on a door-step, with a basket of broken meat! And the most perfect home I ever saw was in a little house into the sweet incense of whose fires went no costly things. A thousand dollars served for a year's living of father, mother, and three children. But the mother was a creator of a home; her relation with her children was the most beautiful I have ever seen; even a dull and commonplace man was lifted up and enabled to do good work for souls, by the atmosphere which this woman created; every inmate of her house involuntarily looked into her face for the key-note of the day; and it always rang clear. From the rose-bud or clover-leaf which, in spite of her hard housework, she always found time to put by our plates at breakfast, down to the essay or story she had on hand to be read or discussed in the evening, there was no intermission of her influence. She has always been and always will be my ideal of a mother, wife, home-maker. If to her quick brain, loving heart, and exquisite tact had been added the appliances of wealth and the enlargements of a wider culture, hers would have been absolutely the ideal home. As it was, it was the best I have ever seen. It is more than twenty years since I crossed its threshold. I do not know whether she is living or not. But, as I see house after house in which fathers and mothers and children are dragging out their lives in a hap-hazard alternation of listless routine and unpleasant collision, I always think with a sigh of that poor little cottage by the seashore, and of the woman who was "the light thereof;" and I find in the faces of many men and children, as plainly written and as sad to see as in the newspaper columns of "Personals," "Wanted, — a home."

www.ingramcontent.com/pod-product-compliance
Lightning Source LLC
LaVergne TN
LVHW050522100826
845148LV00002B/413
* 9 7 8 1 4 2 5 5 2 0 2 2 9 *